THE HEIRESSES OF BUCCLEUCH

This book is gratefully dedicated to two very dear friends: Patrick, Earl of Lauderdale, whose wit, charm, good company, kindness, and generosity have been a source of pleasure to me for well-nigh forty years,

and

Mary S. Hartman, my colleague at Rutgers for more than a quarter of a century, who has taught me that, in history as in life, women matter.

THE HEIRESSES OF BUCCLEUCH:

MARRIAGE, MONEY AND POLITICS
IN SEVENTEENTH-CENTURY BRITAIN

Maurice Lee, Jr.

TUCKWELL PRESS

First published in Great Britain in 1996 by
Tuckwell Press Ltd
The Mill House
Phantassie
East Linton
East Lothian EH40 3DG

A catalogue record for this book is available
on request from the British Library.
The publisher acknowledges subsidy from

towards publication of this volume.

Typeset by Hewer Text Composition Services, Edinburgh
Printed and bound by Cromwell Press,
Broughton Gifford, Melksham, Wiltshire

Contents

Acknowledgements		vi
Foreword: Apologia Pro Libro Suo		vii
Dramatis Personae		x
Family Tables:		
	1. The Family of Buccleuch	xiii
	2. The Leslies	xiv
	3. The Tweeddale–Lauderdale Connection	xv
List of Illustrations		xvi
Prologue: The Tower of London, July 1685		1
1 The Buccleuch Inheritance		4
2 The Wicked Uncle		19
3 Marrying in Haste		31
4 A Beginning and an End		44
5 A Royal Bridegroom		56
6 An Illegal Act of Parliament		79
7 Wife to Prince Perkin		96
Epilogue: The Widowed Duchess		119
Afterword: Closing the Family Album		124
Appendix A: Note on the Sources		127
Appendix B: 'Ugly Meg, or The Robber's Wedding'		131
Glossary		135
Index		137

ACKNOWLEDGEMENTS

I am grateful for the help of many individuals and institutions in the preparation of this book. I could not have written it without having been able to make use of the collections of the Princeton, Rutgers, and Edinburgh University libraries, the Folger Shakespeare Library, the New York Public Library, the British Library, the National Library of Scotland, and the Scottish Record Office. His Grace the Duke of Buccleuch kindly gave permission to use the Buccleuch manuscripts in the Scottish Record Office. Portions of Chapters 5 and 6 appeared in different form in *Albion* in 1993; I am grateful to the editor, Dr. Michael Moore, for permission to reprint. I have benefited from the conversation and/or advice of Professor Bruce Lenman, Dr. Roy Porter, and Dr. Barry Coward. Dr. Jenny Wormald, Lady Antonia Fraser, Dr. Mary S. Hartman, and Ms. Marlie Wasserman were good enough to read portions of the manuscript and give me their advice, to my considerable advantage. Dr. Kathleen Colquhoun took time off from her own researches in Edinburgh to do some preliminary searching of manuscript collections for me. Ms. Nancy Baker, then a student at Rutgers, was a most helpful research assistant. The book is the better for the attentions of all these kind people; its shortcomings are entirely my own. Finally my thanks go to Dr. John Tuckwell of Tuckwell Press for his enthusiasm and encouragement.

FOREWORD: *Apologia Pro Libro Suo*

In its earliest and most enduring form history was storytelling: *historia*. The tales told were of many different sorts: heroic, patriotic, hagiographical, cautionary, often recounted with an admixture of fantasy. In the modern era history became 'scientific', as we all know. Fantasy was banished, only to reappear as authorial bias. The finger of God disappeared as a causative force, to be replaced by the mundane calculations of human beings, mostly men, and mostly men in high places at that. But since history was still the actions of (mostly) men, it was still storytelling. Then, in the twentieth century, came a great change. The bright lights of the historical profession, those who made their living by teaching and writing history, turned their backs upon storytelling. To describe a work of history as *histoire événementielle* was to condemn it. What mattered to the historian—or what should matter—were those vast impersonal forces that determined the course of those events: in the hands of the more circumspect, what events *could* take place, in the hands of the truly deterministic, what events *would* take place. It really did not matter whether the dictator who emerged in 1793 was named Robespierre or Danton, or he of 1799 Napoleon or Moreau. History ceased to be storytelling; it became analysis, wonderfully aided by both the theories of the social scientists and the new technology which made the performance of the requisite mathematical and statistical operations so much quicker and easier. The quantifier reigned supreme.

So storytelling receded from what the dominant analysts like to call the 'cutting edge' of historical investigation. But it did not disappear; it simply changed its venue, and became the province of the learned 'amateurs', the Barbara Tuchmans and C. V. Wedgwoods, who practised their art—and it was an art, not a science, in their hands—outside of academe. There always remained, of course, a traditionalist coterie inside the university, whose members kept on writing narrative history, mostly political, and biography. Their scientific-minded colleagues held them in a certain amount of contempt, not unmixed with jealousy, because their old-fashioned books frequently sold better than those of the number-crunchers. Then, a little over ten years ago, came a startling development. One of the leading practitioners of analytical history—leading in the sense of both the influence and the sales of his work—Lawrence Stone, spoke favourably of a revival of narrative, provided it was 'thick description', interspersed with analysis. Storytelling was all right again, though still not, one suspects, back on the cutting edge. But not storytelling for its own sake. The tale must have wider implications, like that of the accused miller told by Carlo Ginzberg in *The Cheese and the Worms*, or those of the middle-class ladies had up for murder in my colleague Mary Hartman's *Victorian Murderesses*.

This historian, an unrepentant writer of narrative for forty years, proposes to violate the new rule and tell a story mostly for its own sake. It is a tale of two girls, Mary and Anna Scott, the daughters of Francis Scott, second earl of Buccleuch, who died in 1651 when Mary was four years old, and Anna less than a year, leaving behind him an entailed estate with the largest income in Scotland. They inherited the fortune successively, because Mary died young and childless. For at least twenty-five years after Earl Francis's death the ultimate disposition of the estate was uncertain, and it was not for nearly forty years that all the loose ends were tied up. So this is the story of Mary and Anna, their marriages, their husbands, and their ultimate destiny. It is also the story of their mother, the much-married Margaret Leslie, the progenitrix of three aristocratic houses, of their father Earl Francis, who created the entail that caused so much trouble, of their kindly stepfather David, earl of Wemyss, of their allegedly wicked uncle, John Hay, earl of Tweeddale, the husband of Earl Francis's sister, of their undeniably greedy uncle John Leslie, earl of Rothes, and of many others besides: King Charles II, General Monck, who restored him to his throne, Oliver Cromwell and his son Richard, John Maitland, earl of Lauderdale, the iron-fisted dictator of Scotland, and other assorted politicians, both Scottish and English. And many, many members of the family of Scott. It is, for the most part, a story about money and the pursuit of money, an unedifying tale of aristocratic greed and chicanery, family quarrels, the making of marriages and their consequences, and political intrigue of all kinds, played out against a background of political and social turmoil in its early phases, and then of the deceptive and uncertain calm of the restored monarchy.

The story has been told once before, though incompletely, by that tireless antiquarian Sir William Fraser, who in the later nineteenth century wrote the history of so many Scottish aristocratic families. You can find it in his two volumes on *The Scotts of Buccleuch*, if you can find the work at all; it is virtually unobtainable in the United States except in a few research libraries. My debt to Fraser will be obvious to all those familiar with his book. My account is based on much else besides, including many sources, both printed and manuscript, that Fraser did not use (see Appendix A: Note on the Sources). It is also the product of the information accumulated in the course of forty years of study of and writing about the history of sixteenth- and seventeenth-century Scotland and England. For the first, and thus far the only, time in my career as a practising historian, I have opted to eschew scholarly apparatus. This decision will no doubt provoke criticism. So be it.

A word must be said about money, since it figures so extensively in this story. The English pound sterling was worth twelve Scottish pounds. The Scottish merk (English mark) was worth two-thirds of a pound. It is difficult to calculate modern equivalents. The best advice I have, given in 1993 by Dr. Barry Coward, an expert on these matters for the seventeenth century, is that an English pound of the mid-seventeenth century would be worth about £200 now; so the Scottish pound would be slightly under £17 and the merk slightly over £11 (in dollars at the time of writing, $300, $25.50 and $15.50 respectively). Figures are always given in Scottish money unless otherwise indicated, except in Chapter 7 and the Epilogue, where they are given in sterling.

Here, then, is the story of the heiresses of Buccleuch. I tell the tale mostly for its own sake—'thin description', it might be called, though I pause from time to time to discuss matters that the tale illustrates, such as aristocratic marital arrangements, Scottish politics, and the Caroline court. Different readers will draw different conclusions. My chief hope is that, as they close the book, they will all conclude that they have read a good history in the old, original sense of the word.

DRAMATIS PERSONAE

THE SCOTTISH PLAYERS

1. The Buccleuchs and their kin

Walter Scott, 1st earl of Buccleuch (d.1633)
Margaret, Lady Ross, his sister
Alexander Montgomery, earl of Eglinton, her second husband
Francis, 2nd earl of Buccleuch (d. 1651), son of the 1st earl
Margaret Leslie, his wife, later countess of Wemyss (d. 1688)
Jean Scott, his sister (d. 1688)
John Hay, 2nd earl of Tweeddale, her husband (d. 1697)
David Scott, Francis's brother (d. 1648)
Mary Scott, Francis's sister (d. by 1644)
Mary Scott, Francis's daughter (d. 1661)   } THE HEIRESSES
Anna Scott, Francis's younger daughter (d. 1732) }
Walter Scott, later earl of Tarras, Mary's husband (d. 1693)
James (Crofts) Scott, duke of Monmouth, Anna's husband (d. 1685)
John Hay, Lord Yester, son of Jean Scott and Tweeddale
Mary Maitland, his wife
John Maitland, earl (later duke) of Lauderdale, her father (d. 1682)
Anne Home, his first wife (d. 1671)
Elizabeth Murray, countess of Dysart, his second wife
Charles Maitland, Lord Halton, his brother
Charles Seton, earl of Dunfermline, uncle to Tweeddale and Lauderdale
John Leslie, earl (later duke) of Rothes, Margaret Leslie's brother
Alexander Leslie, Lord Balgonie, Margaret Leslie's son by her first marriage
Catherine Leslie, her daughter by her first marriage
George, Lord Melville, Catherine's husband
David, earl of Wemyss, Margaret Leslie's third husband (d. 1679)
Lord Elcho (d. 1671), their son
Margaret, later countess of Wemyss, their daughter

2. The tutors to the heiresses

Sir William Scott of Harden (d. 1655)
William Scott of Harden, his son
Sir Gideon Scott of Haychesters, his second son, father to Tarras
Patrick Scott of Thirlestane, his third son
Sir John Scott of Scotstarvit

William Scott of Clerkington
John Scott of Gorrenberry
Lawrence Scott of Bavielaw
Gilbert Elliott of Stobs

3. *Other Scottish players*

Walter Scott of Satchells, poet
James Livingstone, earl of Callander, uncle to Tweeddale
Gilbert Hay, earl of Erroll, Tweeddale's kinsman
Sir John Gilmour, lawyer, president of the court of session
Sir John Nisbet, lawyer, later lord advocate, Tweeddale's legal adviser
Sir Thomas Wallace, lawyer, Lady Wemyss's legal adviser
William Cunningham, earl of Glencairn, lord chancellor of Scotland
John Middleton, earl of Middleton, Scottish high commissioner
Sir Robert Moray, friend to Tweeddale, Lauderdale, and King Charles
Thomas Ross, Monmouth's tutor
William, Lord Cochrane, one of Monmouth's curators
John Lindsay, earl of Crawford, Rothes' father-in-law
William, Lord Bellenden, Scottish Treasurer-depute
George Mackenzie of Tarbat, later earl of Cromartie, friend to Anna
William Sharp, Lauderdale's Edinburgh business agent

The English Players

Oliver Cromwell, Lord Protector
Richard, his son, also Lord Protector
General George Monck, high commissioner in Scotland
King Charles II, Monmouth's father
James, duke of York, later James II, Charles's brother
Lucy Walter, Monmouth's mother
Edward Hyde, earl of Clarendon, lord chancellor of England
Sir Henry Bennet, later earl of Arlington, secretary of state
Anthony Ashley Cooper, earl of Shaftesbury, Monmouth's political patron
Sir Thomas Clifford, lord treasurer
George Villiers, duke of Buckingham, friend to King Charles
Barbara Villiers, Lady Castlemaine, later duchess of Cleveland, Charles's mistress
Leoline Jenkins, lawyer, later secretary of state
Eleanor Needham, Monmouth's mistress
Lady Henrietta Wentworth, Monmouth's mistress
Sir Stephen Fox, the Monmouths' business agent
Charles, Lord Cornwallis, his son-in-law, later second husband to Anna

1. The Family of Buccleuch

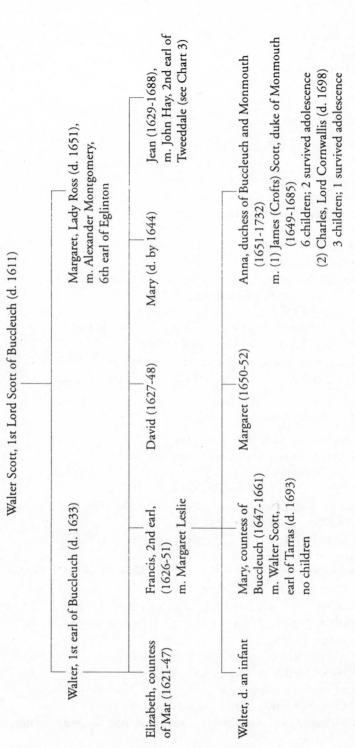

Walter Scott, 1st Lord Scott of Buccleuch (d. 1611)

Walter, 1st earl of Buccleuch (d. 1633)

Margaret, Lady Ross (d. 1651),
m. Alexander Montgomery,
6th earl of Eglinton

Elizabeth, countess
of Mar (1621-47)

Francis, 2nd earl,
(1626-51)
m. Margaret Leslie

David (1627-48)

Jean (1629-1688),
m. John Hay, 2nd earl of
Tweeddale (see Chart 3)

Walter, d. an infant

Mary, countess of
Buccleuch (1647-1661)
m. Walter Scott,
earl of Tarras (d. 1693)
no children

Margaret (1650-52)

Mary (d. by 1644)

Anna, duchess of Buccleuch and Monmouth
(1651-1732)
m. (1) James (Crofts) Scott, duke of Monmouth
(1649-1685)
   6 children; 2 survived adolescence
   (2) Charles, Lord Cornwallis (d. 1698)
   3 children; 1 survived adolescence

2. The Leslies

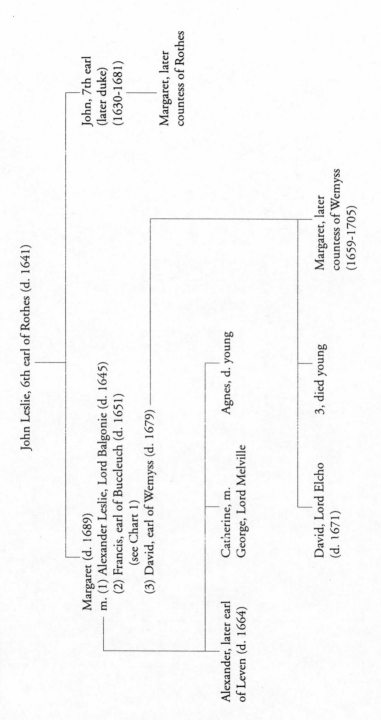

John Leslie, 6th earl of Rothes (d. 1641)

Margaret (d. 1689)
m. (1) Alexander Leslie, Lord Balgonie (d. 1645)
    (2) Francis, earl of Buccleuch (d. 1651)
        (see Chart 1)
    (3) David, earl of Wemyss (d. 1679)

John, 7th earl
(later duke)
(1630-1681)

Margaret, later
countess of Rothes

Alexander, later earl
of Leven (d. 1664)

Catherine, m.
George, Lord Melville

Agnes, d. young

Margaret, later
countess of Wemyss
(1659-1705)

David, Lord Elcho
(d. 1671)

3, died young

3. The Tweeddale – Lauderdale Connection

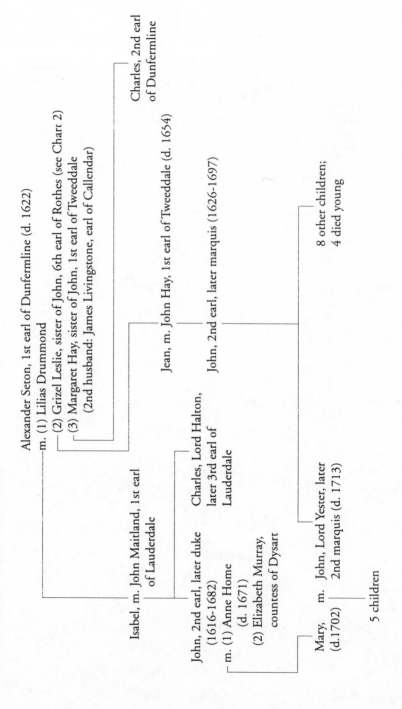

Alexander Seton, 1st earl of Dunfermline (d. 1622)
m. (1) Lilias Drummond
(2) Grizel Leslie, sister of John, 6th earl of Rothes (see Chart 2)
(3) Margaret Hay, sister of John, 1st earl of Tweeddale
(2nd husband: James Livingstone, earl of Callendar)

Charles, 2nd earl
of Dunfermline

Jean, m. John Hay, 1st earl of Tweeddale (d. 1654)

John, 2nd earl, later marquis (1626-1697)

Isabel, m. John Maitland, 1st earl
of Lauderdale

Charles, Lord Halton,
later 3rd earl of
Lauderdale

John, 2nd earl, later duke
(1616-1682)
m. (1) Anne Home
(d. 1671)
(2) Elizabeth Murray,
countess of Dysart

Mary,   m.   John, Lord Yester, later
(d.1702)   2nd marquis (d. 1713)

8 other children;
4 died young

5 children

ILLUSTRATIONS (between pages 64 and 65)

1. Mary Scott, countess of Buccleuch, 1647–1661
2. Anna Scott, countess, then duchess of Buccleuch, 1651–1732
3. Francis Scott, 2nd earl of Buccleuch, father of Mary and Anna
4. Margaret Leslie, wife of Francis Scott
5. David, 2nd earl of Wemyss
6. John Hay, 2nd earl of Tweeddale
7. John Leslie, 7th earl of Rothes
8. John Maitland, 2nd earl of Lauderdale, and Elizabeth Murray
9. James, duke of Monmouth and Buccleuch
10. James VII and II's medal commemorating Monmouth's rebellion

PROLOGUE:
THE TOWER OF LONDON, JULY 1685

On the night of Monday, July 13, 1685, a famous prisoner was lodged in the Tower of London. He was James Scott, duke of Monmouth and Buccleuch, a king's son who had raised a rebellion against his royal uncle, King James II. His treason did not prosper, and he stood condemned to death as an attainted traitor. Earlier that day he had grovelled to the king for mercy, but there was no mercy. The kindliest of kings could not overlook what Monmouth had done, not only claiming James's crown but also calling him an incendiary, an assassin, and a fratricide, and James II was not a forgiving man. Though Monmouth did not know it, he had less than two days to live.

On that same Monday evening Monmouth had a visitor: his wife of twenty-two years, Anna Scott, duchess of Buccleuch in her own right. Monmouth had not seen her for over a year and a half. When Monmouth proclaimed himself king, James ordered that his and Anna's children be held in the Tower; Anna voluntarily accompanied them, to make it perfectly clear that she had nothing to do with her husband's treason. Monmouth had long since ceased to care for her, if indeed he ever had. He flaunted his mistresses and his bastards under her nose, and of late he had been living with the last of them, Lady Henrietta Wentworth. Whatever Anna may have felt about Monmouth, she kept her nerves under control and her wits about her, because her visit had a desperately important purpose, one for which she needed an impeccable witness. So she went to her husband in the company of Henry Hyde, earl of Clarendon, Lord Privy Seal, an important member of James's government and his *quondam* brother-in-law. What was at stake was the future of Anna's children, and of the great Buccleuch inheritance.

Anna's own grip on the Buccleuch estates was not in jeopardy. She held them in her own right, as heir to her father, Francis Scott, earl of Buccleuch, and her elder sister Mary. But her husband was already attainted by act of parliament in England and would certainly be forfeited in Scotland. By law his children shared his guilty blood and would lose their right to inherit their mother's lands unless the king decided otherwise. So it was imperative that Monmouth tell Anna in front of Clarendon that she and their children had no part in his treason. Only thus could King James be persuaded to hold the children harmless.

The interview did not go well. Monmouth was coolly polite to Anna, but the sight of Clarendon revived his faint hope of life, and he cast about for arguments that might induce the earl to persuade James to pardon him. Anna finally interrupted his pitiful performance to ask him point-blank if she had ever given her assent to his behaviour in recent years, or done anything to displease him save to complain of his mistresses and his disobedience to the late King Charles II, his father. Monmouth replied in a distracted and offhand fashion that she had always been a dutiful wife and a good mother, and had always advised him to obey King Charles. This perfunctory response was not what Anna wanted at all.

Two days later, however, it was different. On the morning of the execution Anna came with the children for a final farewell. Now, in the presence of four bishops whom the king had appointed to attend him to the scaffold, and with the children 'all crying about him', Monmouth repeated his statement of Monday and added that 'she knew nothing of his last design, not having heard from himself a year before, which was his own fault, and no unkindness in her, because she knew not how to direct her letters to him'. He went on to adjure her to 'continue her kindness and care to his poor children'. At that Anna's nerves finally snapped. She fell on her knees, began to cry, begged his pardon if she had ever offended him, and 'fell into a swoon out of which they had much ado to raise her up'. A few hours later her husband, praising Lady Henrietta Wentworth to the last, laid his head on the block, where the executioner bungled his job but eventually turned Anna into a widow. She was thirty-four years old. The sorrows of that dreadful summer were not yet over. Within a month Anna lost her only daughter, aged ten. King James ordered that 'the late duchess of Monmouth' be permitted to bury the child in Westminster Abbey if she wished—the little girl was King Charles's granddaughter, after all—and this was done.

'The late duchess of Monmouth': an ominous but accurate phrase. Monmouth's English titles were gone, destroyed by the English parliament's act of attainder. Anna had every reason to hope, however, that her family would not suffer shipwreck. 'His Majesty,' wrote the author of the account already quoted, 'is exceedingly satisfied with her conduct and deportment all along, and has assured her that he will take . . . care of her and her children'. And so he did. In January 1686 he returned Moor Park, the country house she and Monmouth had much enjoyed, which had gone to the crown owing to the attainder. The forms of restitution were carefully followed. After Monmouth was forfeited in Scotland Anna surrendered her honours and estates into the king's hands, and received a charter of regrant to herself, her eldest son James, earl of Dalkeith, and his heirs-male, and then to the next heirs as stipulated in the entail made by her father, of all that she had brought to the marriage, the great Buccleuch inheritance, and more, for the earldom she had inherited was now a dukedom. King James, wrote Anna, was very kind, 'and indeed has ever shown me much favor in what concerns me'. She had reason to be content: her children's future was secure. The king's charter, which was dated November 17, 1687, rang down the curtain on the drama of the heiresses of Buccleuch. The curtain had gone up a little over thirty-seven years earlier, in June 1650, before Anna had even been born.

1

The Buccleuch Inheritance

D uchess Anna's family, the Scotts of Buccleuch, came from the area known as 'the borders', that part of Scotland adjacent to the English frontier. The Scotts had a long history, dating back to at least the late thirteenth century, when Richard Scott, the possessor of the manor house of Buccleuch, swore allegiance to King Edward I, the English invader who claimed suzerainty over Scotland, in order to hang onto his lands. For the next three hundred years proximity to the 'auld enemy', England, determined the lifestyle of the Scott family. They were not like their ancestor, Richard: they were among the 'riding' clans, who made a habit of going on cattle raids in England. On the whole they did very well, making their way up in the world by being (mostly) loyal to the Scottish crown and holding their own in the incessant fighting against both the English and their Scottish neighbours that characterised the border. We have a romantic image of the border clans and their way of life, which we owe to the family genius, Sir Walter Scott. He was fascinated by the history of his family and his region, and he wrote of his ancestors as a race of hardy, gallant fighting men. So they were—and ruffianly, dishonest, and savage too, often enough.

It was Anna's great-grandfather who decisively altered the family's fortunes. He was also called Walter, a common name amongst the Scotts. He inherited the family estates as a boy of nine in 1574. This was normal for the lairds of Buccleuch: like the monarchs of the Stewart dynasty, most of them succeeded as minors. Walter grew up like his forebears, feuding with many of his neighbours and even, briefly, with some of his kinfolk. In his youth he participated fully in the family's traditional occupation of raiding in England, but he recognised sooner than most of the other border clan chiefs that the traditional way of life of the great border families was about to change beyond recognition. In the later sixteenth century England was no longer the enemy. For a generation the ties between England

and Scotland forged by their common Protestantism had become steadily closer, and Scottish governments, beginning in the late 1560s, were more concerned to stop border raiding than, as in the past, to encourage it. By the 1590s the possibility that Scotland's king, James VI, would inherit the throne of the ageing Queen Elizabeth of England was becoming stronger every year. James was not a man of violence, and he detested aristocratic feuds. There was apt to be far more profit in future for the Scotts in loyalty and obedience to the crown and winning royal favour than in pursuing the traditional way of life. Buccleuch did not become a carpet knight, of course, but he found ways of turning his propensity for violent action into legitimate channels as a border official and, after 1604, as commander of a Scottish regiment in the Netherlands in the service of Prince Maurice of Orange. He reaped his rewards. In 1594 he received the great bulk of the estates of the forfeited earl of Bothwell, scattered all across the borders from Dumfriesshire to Berwickshire, including the lands and lordship of Liddesdale, of which he became keeper. Buccleuch got all this, said King James in his charter, for his 'good, faithful, and thankful service . . . in pacifying the Borders and middle regions of the Marches of this our kingdom and putting down the insolence and disobedience of our subjects dwelling there'. The border robber had become an important law-enforcement officer: a remarkable change. He also became a great magnate. He received a peerage at the time of the large-scale handing-out of such largesse at the parliamentary session of 1606: Lord Scott of Buccleuch. King James well knew the value of this tough, clever thief-turned-policeman. Buccleuch had only five years to enjoy his new eminence; he died in 1611.

The first Lord Scott was the stuff of legend—the subject of one of the most famous of border ballads because he organised one of the greatest jailbreaks of all time, the extrication of the notorious thief Kinmont Willie Armstrong from the clutches of the English commander of Carlisle Castle in 1596. His son, also a Walter, achieved nothing so spectacular as that, and after 1603 there was no scope for such derring-do anyway. But in many ways he was very like his father—a tough border policeman in the 1620s and a soldier in the Netherlands, off and on, after 1627. He was also extravagant, as befitted a great landowner who married an earl's daughter, and in 1619 he became an earl himself, less, perhaps, for his own services than for those of his predecessors, as King James's patent rather slightingly reminded him. This Walter Scott was a great purchaser of land. Between 1612 and 1620 he spent over £250,000 on land. In fact he got in over his head, but he had the good sense to entrust his affairs to his kinsman Sir William Scott of Harden, a very talented man of business who may have learned his trade from his father-in-law, Sir Gideon Murray of Elibank, the Treasurer-depute from 1612 until his suicide in 1621.* Harden made considerable headway in straightening out the earl's affairs. When the earl died, his debts amounted to some £175,000, by no means an unmanageable sum, given a rent-roll (income from rents) in the neighbourhood of £90,000 and some £90,000 more in debts owing to the estate. The fortunes of the Buccleuch family were still on the rise.

Earl Walter died in 1633 at the comparatively early age of forty-six, and left behind him a brood of orphans: his wife had died shortly after giving birth to their last child two years earlier. The eldest was a girl of twelve; the new earl, Francis, was only seven. The earl's will named eight Scotts as tutors[†] to his children, including the invaluable Harden and Sir John Scott of Scotstarvit, a clever and malicious troublemaker who was an important chancery official and stood well with the king. The children were all carefully provided for. The daughters' dowries were stipulated in the earl's marriage contract, and the younger son David received various lands by a spe-

---

* The marriage of William Scott of Harden to Elibank's daughter is itself the subject of a romantic tale, that of muckle-mouth Meg. According to the story Elibank seized Harden as he was attempting, in customary border fashion, to steal Elibank's cattle. Elibank brought him home and proposed to hang him, but was stopped by his wife, who pointed out that their daughter was the ugliest woman in four counties: here was a chance to provide her with a handsome and otherwise well-endowed husband. Meg was so ugly that Harden positively refused to marry her until the rope was put round his neck, at which point he changed his mind; the marriage contract was immediately written down on the head of a drum. The story is, alas, a myth. Harden's wife was named Agnes, and there are two marriage contracts, indicating a long and careful negotiation; this was no drumhead wedding. But the story is *ben trovato*, and was the subject of a poem written in the later eighteenth century by Lady Louisa Stuart, the daughter of George III's favourite Lord Bute, which reflects what a witty and acerbic critic thought about aristocratic marriages. See Appendix B.

† Under Scots law, which here followed the principles of Roman law, tutors were necessary to administer the estate of an heir who was a child. If tutors were not named in the father's will, they could be appointed by the courts or the crown. When the child reached 'minority', defined as age 12 for girls, 14 for boys, s/he might ask the courts to name curators to replace the tutors and act with the minor until s/he reached majority.

cial bond. Since the death of their mother the children had been living with their aunt, Margaret Scott, Lady Ross, now a widow, and they stayed with her. She received the not-very-munificent sum of £2,616 13s. 4d. in 1633 for caring for them; the young earl had to beg the tutors for pocket money to reward the servants. When he was ten he and David were sent to St. Andrews to be educated; once again they were kept on short rations. But the earl did not complain; frugality was evidently a part of his nature. There is no question of his affection for his aunt. When he was on his first military adventure, at the age of seventeen, he wrote an endearing little note to her, speaking of his 'true zeal and love unchangeable toward your ladyship, whose unrequitable favors shall never be forgotten'. He added in a postscript that her husband was well: 'I was with him yesterday'. Lady Ross had remarried, to a major player in the confused politics of the 1640s, Alexander Montgomery, earl of Eglinton, a respected soldier known as Greysteel. Eglinton was, and remained, a political follower of the marquis of Argyll, the dominant figure in the party opposed to King Charles I. He was to be an important influence in the life of his new nephew, who, the evidence suggests, followed Eglinton's political lead during his short life.

Francis Scott is a shadowy figure. Because he died so young it is difficult to assess him. He was thrust into politics early because of his great position, interrupting his studies at the age of fourteen in 1641 to be present at parliament. At sixteen he left St. Andrews and became a colonel in the army in order to raise a regiment from his own estates. This army was being raised by the men in control of the Scottish government in consequence of the agreement they had made in 1643 with the leaders of the English rebels against King Charles, the treaty known as the Solemn League and Covenant. The Scots were about to intervene in the English civil war on the side of the king's enemies.

It is not surprising that Francis Scott should have become a Covenanter.* He and his had no reason to love King Charles. He had

---

* 'Covenanter' is a confusing term, since there are two 'Covenants' in this period. The National Covenant of 1638 was signed by the vast majority of the important people in Scotland out of dislike of the policies of King Charles; the movement was triggered by Charles's attempt in 1637 to impose a new liturgy which the Scots regarded as Popish. Then there was the Solemn League and Covenant, of which many of the 'Covenanters' of 1638 disapproved—the earl of Montrose, for instance, who in 1644 would rise in arms for King Charles. After 1643 the term 'Covenanter' applies to those who, like Francis, supported both Covenants.

become the king's ward in spite of the fact that his ancestral barony of Branxholm and the Bothwell estates had been exempted from the obligations of wardship, on account of a minor piece of property in Ettrick Forest which, too late, he sold. The king granted the wardship to the Scottish secretary of state, the earl of Stirling, who certainly needed money: he had impoverished himself in the failed Nova Scotia colonising venture. Francis and his tutors later had to buy out Stirling's widow for a sum in excess of £16,000. What was worse, the king forced Francis to surrender a substantial part of the Bothwell estates to the dead earl's eldest son. This was a long and complicated business that had begun back in 1627 for reasons that are unclear. In 1631 King Charles decreed that Buccleuch should give up one third of what he had acquired. The process of valuation then began. There was no final settlement until 1647, at which point Francis had to pay £50,000, mostly arrears of rent, and in return got a charter for what remained, mostly the lordship of Liddesdale. The whole business had been very costly and irritating, and, to the Scotts, thoroughly unjust. Small wonder that Earl Francis, in the king's words, written when the boy was only twelve, 'had been induced to adhere to the courses of the Covenanters, which much displeased us'. In spite of all their difficulties in this business, however, Francis's tutors managed so well that by 1642 they had not only cleared up Earl Walter's debts but also could spend the enormous sum of £320,000 to purchase the lands and lordship of Dalkeith, a great estate belonging to the bankrupt earl of Morton, a hugely valuable acquisition, and £70,000 more completing the process, begun by Earl Walter, of acquiring the barony of Langholm.

Earl Francis—or his tutors—bought property like his father, but otherwise there was little resemblance. Francis raised troops, and his regiment did well in such actions as the storming of Newcastle in October 1644, but he showed little taste for soldiering. He worked intermittently at border administration, mainly in order to prevent destruction on his own estates, but after 1648 and the worsening of relations with the English this became very difficult. The first family poet, Walter Scott of Satchells, who wrote a family history in execrable verse at the end of the seventeenth century, stated that 'His father's acts were all military/ And he was much inclined to study'. Francis held to a steady line politically, the same line as that of his uncle Eglinton. As became a wealthy man, he supported the Covenanters' military effort with loans and contributions. In 1646 he became a member of the committee of estates, the executive committee that ran the government when parliament was not in session, as did Eglinton, and he remained on the committee for the remaining five years of his life. But there is no record of any political action on his part before 1650 save once, in March 1649, when he protested against the parliamentary act abolishing lay patronage in the church as derogating from aristocratic rights. He actually walked out of parliament. But he was back by June.

The last two years of Francis's life are the most interesting. They are also irritatingly obscure. In the summer of 1646 Francis, aged nineteen, had taken a wife. The choice was curious: a widow lady with two children. She was about five years older than he, far from beautiful, and she brought little by way of wealth to the marriage. But she was well connected. Her name was Margaret Leslie; her brother was earl of Rothes, of an ancient and financially embarrassed Fife family, and her sister was married to Eglinton's son and heir. She was the widow of another Leslie, Alexander, Lord Balgonie, the son of the Covenanting army commander, Alexander Leslie, earl of Leven. Her wedding to Francis was hardly lavish: she had to borrow the earl of Crawford's silver plate, and at the end paid off the servants, 'fiddlers, pipers, and others', to the tune of £375 14s. over and above the drink money 'because there was too little thereof'. (But £24 was spent on three dozen spears for running at the glove, a variant of the more common running at the ring.)

Margaret Leslie was a remarkable woman, possessed of an iron will and determination, who knew what she wanted and generally got it. And she knew how to please her husbands. Francis wrote to her in 1648 that 'your sweet company is the greatest, yea, I may justly say, the only contentment I have on earth', and there is no reason to doubt him. She gave him four children in their five years of marriage, three daughters and one son, born in November 1648. Unhappily the little boy died in the spring of 1650—'my lord and his lady take it very grievously, the death of their son,' wrote Francis's beloved Aunt Margaret on May 8 of that year. That misfortune prompted Francis to a decision which was to have enormous consequences: he would execute a band of tailzie (entail) with respect to his estates.

Francis's immediate living relatives were few. He had two daughters, Mary, born August 31, 1647—the date will be important—and

Margaret, born in March 1650, just before the death of her brother. Anna, the third daughter, would be born in 1651. All but one of Francis's brothers and sisters were dead. His eldest sister had made a splendid marriage to the heir of the earldom of Mar and had died childless in her twenties. His youngest sister Mary did not live to see her fourteenth birthday. Saddest of all to him, his brother David, his fellow student in St. Andrews, died unmarried in July 1648. Only his sister Jean was still alive. In 1650 she was twenty-one years old and had been married for six years to John Hay, Lord Yester, the heir to the earldom of Tweeddale. She had already given him a son; she would give him many more, and many daughters too.

On June 14, 1650, Francis entailed his estate. The document was for the most part very precisely drawn. The heirs male of Francis's body, if there were any, would succeed him; if there were none, then the eldest heir female (singular) of his body, whom failing, Lady Jean his sister and her heirs male, or eldest heir female. If all these failed, the heir would be anyone he might nominate during his lifetime—he named no one. If a woman succeeded to the estate, she had to marry a Scott, or someone who would take the name of Scott and assume the arms of the family of Buccleuch.* There were other restrictions on a female successor. She could not sell any part of the estate, or set a lease for any longer than one year after her death. She could raise capital by mortgages if necessary, up to a limit of 100,000 merks, but only if the income from the mortgaged land covered the interest payments.† On no account could she alter the entail. If she tried, she would *ipso facto* forfeit her right to possess the estate, and it would go to the next heir.

Having done this, Earl Francis made his will, dated the following day, June 15, 1650. Did he believe that he might die young? It is impossible to say. There is some evidence of bad health; his brother-in-law, in a memoir written more than twenty years later, remarked that in 1650 Francis suffered from a 'decay'—whatever that might be—that killed him in the following year. Francis's predilection for

---

* Name-changing was far from unprecedented. The earl of Eglinton, Francis's much-admired uncle by marriage, had been born Alexander Seton, the third son of Robert Seton, earl of Winton. His mother was a Montgomery, and he changed his name to Montgomery when he acquired the Montgomery earldom.

† A Scottish landowner who raised capital by mortgaging land retained the income from the land; the lender acquired it only if the landowner defaulted on the loan.

study rather than things military might be an indication that he was not robust. And the track record of the Scotts was bad: so many of them did die young. Perhaps Francis was merely being prudent. That he did not expect to die immediately is suggested by his naming in his will of his non-existent eldest son as the heir to his personal estate; next came his daughters; if he should die childless his widow would inherit his movables. He ordered his obligations to be met, including the lump sums provided for his daughters in his marriage contract (assuming there was a male heir). They were one-third larger than the sums provided in his father's marriage contract thirty years earlier: an indication of the growth in the value of the estate. Like his father, he named a council of tutors for his children. As was customary in such situations, they were members of the family: all Scotts save for Margaret his widow and two Elliots. The tutors could do nothing in Margaret's absence. But if she remarried she ceased to be a member of the council. In that event three Scotts were singled out: Scotstarvit, William Scott of Clerkington—like Scotstarvit a member of the court of session, Scotland's highest court—and the indispensable (and elderly) Harden. At least two of these three had to be present for the council of tutors, whose quorum was five, to act. (These details are tedious, but they become vital later on.) Lady Margaret lost her place on the council if she remarried, on the ground that she might place the interests of her new husband and his family above those of the heirs. For the same reason Francis did not name his brother-in-law, Lord Yester, to the council. It was customary to exclude the next prospective heir from the guardianship of children who inherited property; so Yester was not appointed, even though it was his wife, not he, who stood to inherit if the children should die without issue. But Yester, along with Francis's other brother-in-law, Rothes, and six other nobles, including Eglinton, were named as overseers, which meant that they might lodge protests with the appropriate authorities if they believed that the tutors were abusing their trust.

Francis completed these vitally important personal arrangements at a time when he was becoming more actively involved in politics. The four years of Francis's adult life were among the most traumatic and turbulent in Scottish history. Francis turned twenty-one in December 1647. In that month the moderate majority among the Covenanting aristocracy made an agreement with Charles I, who had been defeated in the civil war, and prepared to send the Scottish army to England to restore him to freedom—a complete reversal of the Covenanting government's previous position. The leadership of the church and a minority of nobles—Argyll, Eglinton, and Francis among them—opposed the agreement, known as the Engagement, and were vindicated, after a fashion, when Cromwell's army routed the Scots at Preston in August 1648. The consequence was the execution of the king in January 1649, an event greeted with universal horror in Scotland, where Argyll took the lead in having the dead ruler's son proclaimed as Charles II.

Francis, as a member of Argyll's party, now regularly attended parliament, and was a member of the committee sent to welcome Charles II when he came to Scotland in July 1650 for the first and only time in his life to make his vain attempt to recover his thrones by force from the victorious armies of England, now officially a republic: the Commonwealth. Francis, like his uncle Eglinton, slowly but steadily became more supportive of the king and of the policy of healing the rift within the aristocracy that the Engagement had caused. Such a reconciliation was a matter of life and death for the country: Charles II's arrival in Scotland had provoked an English invasion and another military disaster at the hands of Cromwell at Dunbar in September 1650. Francis raised a regiment for the army, but he did no fighting himself. He was preoccupied with the safety of his young family and the condition of his estates, which were mostly in areas occupied by the invading English. Margaret and the children took refuge in Dundee, where Anna, his third daughter, was born on February 11, 1651. Then, in April, a form of disaster struck Francis with the capture of Eglinton by the English, who ambushed him in his bed—a man was later hanged for betraying his whereabouts—and took him off to prison in England. Francis was rudderless, and his confusion was compounded when Argyll made it plain that he disapproved of the desperate gamble of invading England which Charles now embarked upon. The king's army met its inevitable doom at Worcester in September 1651.

Francis did not go south with the army. Instead, he concentrated on getting his family to safety. As the English General Monck prepared to assault Dundee in August 1651, Francis moved his family to Aberdeen; when that city, too, appeared unsafe, he took them to his brother-in-law Rothes's house in Fife, which was out of the war zone. By October they were back at Dalkeith, where he had the tragic duty of burying his beloved aunt, Lady Eglinton. She had gone to

England to be with her husband, who was being held at Hull, and there she died, on October 5. Her body was shipped back to what was to become the family mausoleum. Dalkeith, though newly acquired, was the grandest residence Francis possessed, and he planned that it should be the family seat. He would not enjoy it long. Shortly after burying his aunt he fell ill. On November 20 he wrote a codicil to his will, adding two more Scotts to the list of tutors, including, fatefully, Harden's second son, Gideon Scott of Haychesters.* Two days later Francis died. He was not yet twenty-five years old.

What sort of man was Earl Francis? After his death he was described as a grave and pious young man who was concerned always to further the cause of godliness, his country's liberty, and the goals of the Solemn League and Covenant. He had taken arms, it was said, to assist the English in 1643 and to defend the kingdom 'when it was overrun by the Irish and unnatural countrymen'—i.e., the royalist marquis of Montrose and his followers—in 1645. This last statement was a considerable stretching of the truth; Francis refused to allow his troop of 300 horse to be used outside his own lands. All this praise was, in fact, special pleading; for reasons to be explained below, it was crucial to persuade the victorious Cromwell, now Lord Protector, that the earl had never been his enemy. Were the tributes justified? Was he really 'good Earl Francis, dead and gone', as the Last Minstrel said? Perhaps. Scott of Satchells, the family poet, suggested that he had odd sexual proclivities—there were examples, Satchells said, from Sardanapalus to Nero—which was why, unlike his forebears, he left only daughters behind him. Good or not, he was dead and gone too soon for many reasons. His country was in turmoil, without a government and in the grip of a conquering army. His estate was enormous: he had a rent-roll, if it could all be collected, of well over £100,000. (To set this figure in context: the rent-roll of the marquis of Huntly in 1665 produced £31,840.) And the heir to this fortune was a little girl, four years old, Mary, now countess of Buccleuch in her own right.

Mary's mother, Margaret Leslie, after five and a half years of marriage and four children, was once again a widow. She had five children from her two marriages, ranging in age from teenagers to an

---

* The modern hamlet from which this title derives is called Highchesters; the *Scots Peerage* calls Gideon 'Highchester'. Since Gideon called himself Haychesters, so will we.

infant, to look after; and, all at once, she found herself without a house. The English occupiers seized Dalkeith and turned it into an office for their commissioners and then a residence for their commanding general in Scotland. This may have happened because the English thought that Dalkeith was crown property, as indeed it had been for a few years in the late 1630s. Once in, however, mistake or not, they did not get out, in spite of Countess Mary's tutors' protests, though Monck, during his residence there as head of the Scottish administration from 1654 to 1660, paid rent: £110 sterling (£1,320) for the park and orchards—and threepence for the house. The family did not recover the property until the Restoration.

So the widowed countess had to find another place to live. She took up residence with the children at Sheriffhall, near Dalkeith, which was part of the property Earl Francis had settled on her for life when they were married. Her expenses were considerable. She had not only to move but also to bury her husband and, sadly, one of their little daughters, her namesake, who died in 1652. The tutors authorised a cash payment of £10,000 and an allowance of £4,800 a year, to be derived from the lease of the coal mines at Sheriffhall. This was almost twice as much as Lady Ross had received to look after more children in 1633, but it did not strike Margaret as very generous. Nor did she fancy eking out an existence at Sheriffhall subject to the constant interference of the tutors. Though her husband's will had provided that they could not act in her absence, this was no guarantee that she could always get them to act as she wished. She wanted another husband, and in slightly more than a year she had one.

David, earl of Wemyss, like Margaret, had buried two spouses. His first wife, who had died in 1649, had given him eleven children, of whom only two daughters had survived. His second marriage, to a sister of Lord Fleming, lasted only two years and was a disaster. She was an extravagant alcoholic who left him, according to John Lamont the diarist, 100,000 merks the poorer. Wemyss buried her in May 1652 and almost at once began to pay court to Margaret. Their dalliance was not prolonged; in January 1653 they were married at Sheriff-hall and went to live in Wemyss Castle in Fife, taking Francis's two small children with them.

Margaret's new husband was a different sort of man from his predecessor. Earl David was forty-two when she married him, an experienced politician and entrepreneur with extensive coal mines and salt pans. His and Francis's politics had been the same. He was a follower of Argyll, did a lot of soldiering—he was the commander of the Covenanting army that Montrose routed at Tippermuir—and opposed the Engagement. Like Francis he was a member of the committee of estates. After 1651, with the English occupation, Wemyss began to eschew politics. He was concerned to protect his position and properties, and his ties with Argyll suggested to him, both before and after 1660, that a low profile was advisable. So in his later years—he died in 1679—he concentrated on developing his properties, building a harbour to market his coal and salt more readily, and adding an extensive modern wing to his medieval castle where, in 1565, Mary Queen of Scots had first laid eyes on Lord Darnley. He built well and provided well: the wing still stands, and is inhabited by his descendants. He and his countess still stare down from their portraits hanging on their walls, cautious, wary, determined not to be gulled—nothing at all like Mary and Darnley. They were a well-matched pair.

Earl David, for all his toughness in business, was a kindly man who related well to children. His stepdaughters loved and trusted him, and regarded him as their father. Anna, on her first real separation from him when she was twelve and newly married, wrote in a touching little note that 'I have obeyed your lordship's commands in keeping of my lady [her mother] merry', and corresponded with him as long as he lived. He wanted a son, of course; over the next six years Margaret presented him with five children, the last born on New Year's Day, 1659. Three died in infancy, but one who did not was indeed a son. The girl born in 1659 was Margaret's last child. In a space of twenty years she had had twelve, half of whom did not survive infancy. Wemyss's record was sixteen births, three survivors at this point. One of his daughters by his first wife had died at sixteen in 1654, and his and Margaret's son would later die young as well, so that in the end there were only two daughters to give Earl David grandchildren and carry on the Wemyss line. It is a melancholy record, which has suggested to some historians that in this period people did not love their children because they dared not: they were too likely to have to bury them. The argument is unconvincing. Tough-minded though she was, Margaret Leslie loved her children. She, in common with the wives of other Scottish aristocrats, was pregnant as regularly as the wives of lesser mortals, and wept as regularly over her children's graves. Fortunately Margaret had a rugged constitution, which withstood the physical and emotional rigours she endured. Childbearing did not diminish her energy: she outlived Earl David by almost a decade and died in 1688.

Earl David and his new countess began their married life under an alien military regime. Military occupations always cost money, and that of the English in Scotland was no exception. The occupiers, like most others in similar circumstances, intended that the occupied should pay. At the end of the 1650s government expenditure in Scotland came to £3,687,259 9s. 2d., of which almost £3,250,000 represented the costs of the army of occupation. The English did not expect to raise the whole sum from Scotland, but they wanted as much as they could get. In 1652 they set the monthly assessment for the army at £120,000, an annual total of £1,440,000. They never raised anything like that amount from the cess, as it was called, and in 1657 they reduced it to a more realistic £72,000 a month. The monthly levy on the Buccleuch estates was £2058 6s. 8d.—2.77% of the national bill, an enormous contribution. In addition to the cess the new rulers imposed customs and excise duties, the whole paraphernalia of taxation levied in England, on a country far less able to pay. It was a very heavy burden, and it fell most heavily on the landed classes, because they had no way to hide their assets. As a consequence most Scottish aristocrats—the Buccleuchs were an exception—were plunged heavily into debt.

In addition to all these taxes the English proposed to punish, by confiscation or fines, those prominent people who had committed the crime, or blunder, of being on the losing side. The landed aristocracy was a particular target: the English thought to secure the stability of their regime by neutralising potential opponents. Since virtually everyone of any importance in Scotland had been on the losing side at one time or another, this gave the English considerable latitude. Some, like the earl of Lauderdale, currently in the Tower of London after his capture at the battle of Worcester in 1651, had their estates confiscated. Lady Lauderdale was allowed to retain lands with an annual income of £3,600, on which she had to pay an annual tax of 5%. The Buccleuch tutors might well have supposed that the estate would get off lightly. Earl Francis had never been in arms against the English; as a youth he had, in fact, fought with them. He had opposed the Engagement; his behaviour during Charles II's year in Scotland had been discreet in the extreme. They were appalled to discover, in the spring of 1654, that the English government proposed to mulct them of £15,000 sterling—£180,000

Scots—almost double the annual rent-roll, all to be paid by the end of the year, on pain of confiscation of the entire estate. Three of the tutors were also fined: Harden was to pay £3,000, his son Patrick Scott of Thirlestane £2,000, and Scotstarvit £1,500—all sterling.

These penalties were contained in a document called the Act of Pardon and Grace, which closed the books on the Scots' unsuccessful wars against England between 1648 and 1651. Coinciding as it did with the appointment of General Monck, a presbyterian and an ex-royalist, as head of the civil and military establishments in Scotland, it indicated that Cromwell was now prepared to try conciliation rather than repression there. But to the Buccleuch tutors the Act must have seemed cynically named.

Why was the fine so large? What was Earl Francis's offence? It was not difficult to conclude that his chief crime was his wealth; the estate was there to be mulcted. The amount of the fine was outrageous, far more than anyone else was required to pay. The ostensible reason for it was a letter which had gone out over Francis's signature from Aberdeen on August 30, 1651. The circumstances were these. Francis had taken his family from Dundee to Aberdeen earlier that month, as has been said. The committee of estates, of which he was a member, had been meeting at Stirling, but when Monck captured Stirling earlier in August its members moved to Alyth, in Perthshire, about halfway between Stirling and Aberdeen. Monck learned of their whereabouts, and on the night of August 27/28, 1651, sent a raiding party which scooped them all up. Francis and his brother-in-law, Yester, whose family had also been in Dundee and removed to Aberdeen, were on their way to Alyth when they heard the news and hastily returned to Aberdeen.

Scotland was now literally without a government. There were, however, a few members of the committee of estates in Aberdeen, none of any prominence save the earl of Callander, and Francis. They decided to meet in order to write to those few members of the committee still at large inviting them to come to a meeting somewhere, perhaps at the marquis of Huntly's house at Strathbogie, which was far removed from Monck's current area of operations, in order to try to carry on. According to the accounts given in 1654, Francis was importuned to attend this meeting, set for the night of August 30, but he refused: he was determined to get his family (and himself, indeed) out of harm's way. But he did agree, so two of those present later testified, to sign some blank sheets, which could be filled in later. The letter was then composed and sent out; its recipients, among them the earl of Wemyss, were adjured to come to the proposed meeting, at Strathbogie or wherever, 'as you wish religion to be preserved, or this kingdom to be kept from being totally overrun by a handful of bloody traitors'. The last phrase was the one that contained the dynamite: the estate of a man who considered the Lord Protector (as he was in 1654) and his associates bloody traitors should certainly be made to pay for the expression of such deplorable sentiments.

Did Francis know what the letter contained? Or did he in fact sign a set of blank papers—an extremely convenient story to tell in 1654? Two men who were there wrote letters saying that the convenient story was true. One was Sir James Murray, himself a signatory of the letter; the other was Sir Archibald Primrose, the clerk of the committee, the man who took the blank sheets to Francis to be signed. Murray's letter was very circumstantial; it was he, not Primrose, who stated that Primrose procured Francis's signature on the blanks. Primrose himself had to be paid off, to the tune of £1,000, not only to provide his testimony but also to keep quiet about some other business in the committee of estates that would cast doubt on the story that Earl Francis was never anti-English and was always good and pious and a supporter of the Solemn League and Covenant, etc., etc. The line that the English were to believe was that Francis was so inactive in the committee after Charles's return in 1650 as to 'draw upon him the suspicion of one disaffected to the war, and a favorer of those who did not concur therein', as one of the testimonials put it. There is one strong argument in favour of the story of the blanks, and that is the appearance of the letter itself. All the other signatures, a total of ten, are aligned, more or less, in two columns under the closing phrase, 'Your lordship's assured friends', on the right-hand side of the page. Francis's is not; it is on the left, and slightly above that closing phrase. This argues that Murray, and Primrose too, were telling the truth: not everyone who takes a bribe is a liar.

Whatever the truth might be, the Protector's government had the evidence it needed, and the estate was to pay. It was imperative that the tutors make an effort to get this ruinous levy cancelled, or at least reduced. There was only one way to do this: someone had to go to London to persuade Cromwell to be merciful. Enter the wicked uncle: John Hay, Lord Yester, now earl of Tweeddale. The real drama of the Buccleuch heiresses was about to begin.

2

The Wicked Uncle

John Hay, second earl of Tweeddale, is an odd man to cast in the role of wicked uncle. He was always much involved in politics. In the late 1660s and early 1670s, and again after the revolution of 1688, he was a major player, winding up with a marquisate and the office of lord chancellor. As a politician he has had a relatively good press. He 'understood all the interests and concerns of Scotland well', wrote his contemporary, Bishop Gilbert Burnet, who knew him well. 'He had a great stock of knowledge, with a mild and obliging temper. He was of a blameless, or rather an exemplary, life in all respects.' But he was also inclined to swim with the tide. 'He had loose thoughts both of civil and ecclesiastical government, and seemed to think that whatever form soever was uppermost was to be complied with . . . Though he was in all respects the ablest and worthiest man of the nobility, he was too cautious and fearful.' Thus Burnet. One modern scholar has called him selfish and pliant; another, reasonable, intelligent, and inclined to moderate courses. He was a man who in his public life showed some concern for the public interest and welfare as well as his own. This was such a stark contrast with the limitlessly rapacious and self-seeking behaviour of virtually all other aristocratic politicians in Restoration Scotland that it probably accounts for the good marks that most historians have accorded him.

The Hays of Yester were a cadet branch of the great house of Erroll. Like the Scotts, they came from the area between the border and the capital, but they were far removed from the frontier and were not habitually involved in the military larceny that constituted such a large part of the Scotts' way of life. By the fourteenth century they were established in Peeblesshire, where the head of the family became hereditary sheriff, and in East Lothian, the site of Yester House. By the late fifteenth century they were Lords of Parliament: Lords Hay of Yester. John was born in 1626, the eldest son of the eighth Lord Yester, also a John. His mother, Jean Seton, whom her husband described as 'a comely wench and may be a wife to the best in the kingdom', was one of the many daughters of Alexander Seton, earl of Dunfermline and lord chancellor.

This distinguished lawyer and public servant shared to an alarming degree the Scottish aristocracy's enthusiasm for marrying teenage girls. He married three of them in succession; the last, whom he took to his fifty-two-year-old bosom in 1607, when she was fifteen, was John's aunt, Margaret Hay. She presented the ageing chancellor with a son, Charles, who was thus both uncle and first cousin to John, and an unfortunate presence in his life. John's father was much involved in politics from the 1620s onward. He was an early opponent of the policies of Charles I and voted against him in parliament in 1633. One of John's earliest memories was of being taken, aged seven, to see the king at Seton House. Charles kissed the little boy and said to him, 'God make you a better man than your father'.

John's mother died shortly after his birth, and his father did not immediately remarry. So John spent his childhood in the Dunfermline household. In 1638, at the age of twelve, he began a three-year stint at the College of Edinburgh. In the summer of 1642 he was at Nottingham in the company of his uncle-cousin Dunfermline, a gentleman of the royal bedchamber, when King Charles raised his standard and thus touched off the civil war in England, and he accompanied the king to Shrewsbury. Dunfermline had begun as a Covenanter, like most Scottish nobles, but he was now beginning to show royalist sympathies. It did not suit the ardently Covenanting Lord Yester that his son should be infected in this way, so he came to Shrewsbury, collected young John, and took him back to Scotland.

So John became a Covenanter like his father. The ostensible reason for his having accompanied his uncle Dunfermline to the south in 1642 was that he should travel in France. After spending a certain amount of time in close proximity to his father's new wife, a conceited young woman of twenty-four whom Lord Yester, seventeen years a widower, had married at the end of 1641, young John became still more anxious to travel. But now his father would not permit it. War was coming; furthermore, it was time John thought of taking a wife. John went off to war without much enthusiasm. Like Earl Francis, he did not care for soldiering, but he did what was necessary. He took part in some of the campaigning around Newcastle in early 1644 and then came home to the wife who had been selected for him, Earl Francis's sister Jean Scott. He was, he wrote, 'somewhat engaged in affection' to her; he had seen her several times over the past three years, but had never spoken to her! She brought a dowry of 40,000 merks, in return for which she renounced any claims she might have on the estates of her father and mother and her deceased sister Mary. Lord Yester turned over some of his property to them, including Neidpath Castle, where they took up residence in 1646. They were married at Dalkeith on October 19, 1644; he was eighteen, she fifteen. It was to be a very happy marriage.

John's soldiering continued. He was present at the final defeat of the royalist marquis of Montrose at Philiphaugh in 1645. In 1646 he spent a good deal of time at Newcastle with the captive Charles I, who surrendered to the Scottish army early that year. The king took a liking to him; they would discuss the sermons to which his Scottish 'hosts' subjected their royal 'guest', and the king playfully called the young man of twenty 'ruling elder'. When John's father came to Newcastle, Charles was advised to make him an earl, to win his political support if possible. Charles rejoined that he would prefer to make the son an earl, but was told that that would not do, especially as his father had, in John's phrase, 'a proud wife'. So Lord Yester became earl of Tweeddale.

The new earl's politics did not change; he opposed the Engagement, but John supported it, perhaps because of his personal affection for the king. Luckily for him, he was not involved in the military disaster at Preston in 1648; he was at home, awaiting the birth of his son and heir. His support of the Engagement meant political proscription after its failure, but this did not weigh seriously upon him, since his father was still a member of the ruling clique. With the arrival of Charles II in 1650 and the subsequent English invasion of Scotland John went with his family for safety to Dundee, whence he contrived to pay surreptitious visits to Dunfermline when Charles was in residence there. This was important for the future: the new king came to know him. But for the present it signified little enough.

In May 1650 John's father engaged in a legal manoeuvre common among property holders in debt: he transferred title to the Yester and Tweeddale lands to his son. This debt was to be the bane of John Hay's existence for the next forty years and is a major factor in the story of the Buccleuch heiresses, because it was they to whom it was owed. The culprit was John's Uncle Charles. He had inherited a considerable estate from his father, Lord Chancellor Dunfermline, and he proceeded to squander it. He was a *bon vivant*, preferring London to Scotland, a big spender, and a compulsive gambler. 'You was [*sic*] remembered,' wrote Lord Treasurer Rothes in 1665 to Secretary Lauderdale of an official dinner in Edinburgh, 'in Dunfermline's fashion, that is both in drinking and playing.' According to the not-always-reliable Scotstarvit, when Dunfermline had to promise to play no more gambling games, he satisfied his urge by betting on who could 'draw the longest straw out of a stack with the most grains of corn thereon'. Inevitably he began to borrow money, and he persuaded three close kinsmen to be his cautioners, i.e., to promise, with their own estates as security, that the loans would be repaid. One of these was Tweeddale. Dunfermline could not pay his creditors; Tweeddale's estates were seized. John had to mortgage some of his own property to redeem them, and then had to arrange their transfer from his father's name to his. He then had to borrow £40,000 more in order to make good on his father's promise to bail out one of Dunfermline's other two cautioners. He raised the money, with his wealthy brother-in-law Buccleuch as *his* cautioner. He could not repay such a sum; so Buccleuch had to pay John's debt for him. The upshot was that when Earl Francis died in 1651 John owed the Buccleuch estate £40,000—plus, of course, accumulating interest for every year the debt went unpaid. Relief, if it could be had, would come from the Dunfermline estates. This was difficult for John to attempt, however, as long as the dowager countess, Lord Chancellor Dunfermline's widow, was still alive. She was his aunt and his own foster-mother, who had raised him from infancy after his mother's early death, and she had her dower rights. It was a very messy situation, and eventually, so John believed, helped to shorten his father's life. In 1654 the ageing earl had to flee to Berwick, across the English border, to escape his other creditors, and there he died, leaving an enormous debt. The new earl of Tweeddale (we will call him that henceforth) succeeded to a once-prosperous but now badly encumbered estate.

There was one bright spot, however: his wife's prospects. When her brother Earl Francis died, the lives of three little girls were all that stood between her and the vast Buccleuch inheritance and the cancellation of the debt, a number reduced to two with the death of little Margaret in 1652. According to the 'Information of the Condition

of the Family of Buccleuch', later written by Gideon Scott of Haychesters, who loathed him, Tweeddale had confidently expected to be
appointed one of the tutors to the little girls. He showed up at the
first meeting, wrote Haychesters, and was vastly disappointed to discover that he was merely an overseer, a position with no real
power. His financial straits, and his possession of a son whom he
would certainly consider an admirable husband for the little Countess Mary, combined to make him a suspicious figure in the eyes of
the tutors and the girls' mother. Nevertheless, if one believes Haychesters, the tutors did not want to antagonise him. They supplied
him with some £4,000 to satisfy his creditors. Then, in 1654, came
the news of that enormous fine. The tutors were aghast. An appeal
was essential. Someone had to go to London to persuade the Lord
Protector, and the commission he set up for the purpose, to listen favourably to their plea for mitigation. And they chose Tweeddale.

What seems to have swayed the tutors was the argument that
Tweeddale had useful friends among the English occupiers of Scotland, people like Samuel Disbrowe, one of the commissioners for
claims on forfeited estates in Scotland, and George Downing, Scout-
master General of the Forces; such men could get Tweeddale a hearing in Whitehall. Two of the tutors, Clerkington and Patrick Scott
of Langshaw, made this argument; so did John Gilmour, a leading
member of the Edinburgh legal establishment and the dowager
countess's legal adviser. Haychesters later wrote that Clerkington
and Langshaw knew that Tweeddale had influence with the English
because he had used it to keep them off the list of those fined in the
Act of Pardon and Grace. As with so many of Haychesters' statements, there is no independent evidence for this. For whatever reason, the tutors were persuaded; but they would not send
Tweeddale alone. Haychesters would be joined in the commission
with him. The grounds on which they were to plead the case were,
first, that the Protector had been misinformed about the behaviour
of Earl Francis, whose virtuous carriage and lack of enmity to the
English were explicated at some length. The fact that Tweeddale
had been with him in Aberdeen at the time of the writing of the
'bloody traitors' letter was helpful too: he could testify that Francis
had never seen it. In the second place, neither the little countess
nor the tutors were legally able to encumber her estate in order to
pay such a fine. The estate also had other obligations upon it, to
the dowager countess and little Anna, and it had been devastated

and partly occupied by the English—the tutors pointed to the cutting of timber at Dalkeith. Testimonials to the truth of all this were provided. If nevertheless all this was unpersuasive and the fine was to be imposed in whole or in part, the tutors asked to be empowered to borrow money to pay it.

Thus armed, the two commissioners travelled to London, arriving in June 1654. Tweeddale proceeded to make a bad mistake. He resolved to act alone, cutting out Haychesters as much as possible. He wanted all the credit for whatever success the mission might have, and his motive was perfectly transparent. He spelled it out in a letter to the girls' mother, sent from London on July 6, 1654. 'Hitherto I have been made a cipher as to all things concern(ing) that family,' he wrote. He hoped 'that I may for the future have this satisfaction, that by my advice those children may only be disposed of', and that she and Lord Wemyss would regard him and his wife as among their nearest friends. A week later he wrote a similar letter to old Harden, the most influential of the tutors, with a hypocritical P.S. in praise of his son Haychesters, with whom by this time Tweeddale was quarrelling bitterly. Only an instant cancellation of the fine could have justified such tactics, and that was beyond Tweeddale's powers to obtain. Using his connections, he obtained a private interview with Cromwell on June 26, and presented the tutors' petition and supporting material and an additional memorandum asking that any decision respecting mitigation of the fine or extension of the time allowed for payment be made through him. The Scott estate could not possibly pay a fine of £15,000 sterling, he added: its annual income was no more than £60,000 Scots—a considerable understatement. Tweeddale went on to ask that, if Cromwell were minded to reduce or cancel the fines imposed on Harden, Scotstarvit, and Thirlestane, he might be the bearer of that good news also. Cromwell listened carefully, promised another audience at a future date, and referred the tutors' petition to his council, which in turn passed it along to the commission on the fines. There would be no rapid answer.

Within two days Haychesters discovered what Tweeddale had done and expostulated with him. Tweeddale rather lamely said that he had not had time between notification of his meeting with Cromwell and the meeting itself to summon Haychesters. Haychesters did not believe this, and went off to see Henry Lawrence, the president of the Protector's council, to complain about Tweeddale's behaviour and to ask to see the papers that Tweeddale had submitted.

Lawrence refused to show them to Haychesters unless Tweeddale was present. Haychesters grew more suspicious still, but he had no option but to accept Lawrence's terms. So he went to Tweeddale; the two saw Lawrence, and Lawrence showed Haychesters some papers. Haychesters had to concede that all that he saw was perfectly correct. Tweeddale then rounded on him: Haychesters could act by himself from now on, if that was what he wanted. Haychesters replied that if Tweeddale wished to surrender his commission, he could do so by writing to the tutors and getting a release. Until then he would 'continue to attend on him'. Tweeddale went ahead acting by himself anyway, Haychesters complained, and appropriated the lion's share of the expense money to boot.

All this is contained in Haychesters' report to the tutors, dated September 23, 1654; he could not sign Tweeddale's report, he said, because he could not vouch for its accuracy. Whatever Haychesters may have felt about Tweeddale before their joint mission—Tweeddale's letter to Harden suggests that they were not well acquainted—he now hated the earl. Of that there can be no doubt. He was also convinced—or said he was—that Tweeddale was bent on getting the two little girls into his own hands for his own nefarious purposes. So he wrote in a letter to Lady Wemyss on September 25. Tweeddale, he went on, was promoting the calumny that Lady Wemyss was planning to deliver the children into the hands of the enemies of the commonwealth by means of unsuitable marriages in order to prejudice the English authorities against her. Tweeddale had given George Downing a paper indicating that it was Lord Wemyss, one of the recipients of that controversial letter from Aberdeen in August 1651, who had informed on Earl Francis to the English, in order to prejudice the tutors against the earl and, by extension, Lady Wemyss. Nothing was too bad to believe of Tweeddale. He treated his father cruelly and drove him to an early grave. He cleverly contrived the death of Earl Francis's younger brother David in the military campaign of 1648 in order to sweep one more obstacle out of the way of his wife's succession to the Buccleuch inheritance.* Tweed-

---

* In fairness to Haychesters, he did not float this charge. It is contained in a letter *to* him, written in June 1659, at a time when Haychesters' loathing and fear of Tweeddale was at its most intense, as we shall see. The story is inherently improbable—Earl Francis had not yet entailed his estate—and runs counter to the tutors' own evidence. In their petition to Cromwell in 1654 they stated that not only did Francis not fight against the English in 1648, he also dissuaded his brother from doing so. But nothing is too bad to believe of a Truly Wicked Uncle.

dale was evil incarnate. His purpose in seeing Cromwell in private was to ask the Protector to order that the little girls be turned over to him. If they should fall into his hands, it would be all up with them. The heiress would be wedded to his son, and as for little Anna—who knew what fate would befall her?

Not all the tutors believed Haychesters; perhaps if Tweeddale had been successful in his negotiations over the fine, none of them would have. For the moment, however, the fines all officially stood, though in July the Protector's council had issued a statement suggesting that if one third were paid, the rest might well be excused. This pronouncement marked one more step in the policy of conciliation of the people who counted in Scotland that had begun with the Act of Pardon and Grace in April—but it was to be gradual conciliation, in order to maximise the gratitude of the recipients. Tweeddale rather defensively explained in his report to the tutors that he had done no better than he had because it had taken so long to puzzle out the proper channels of approach in the Protector's bureaucracy. But for Haychesters' purposes what the tutors believed about Tweeddale mattered little enough. He had convinced the one person he wanted to convince: Lady Wemyss. From this point on to the end of her days she never ceased to hate and fear her former brother-in-law. He wanted her children—and their money. That is what she saw; that is all she saw. 'There is no less aimed at,' she wrote to Haychesters in September, 'than the ruin of my young children, and the putting you all that has [*sic*] lawful power out of your station therein.' Haychesters fed her fears. For he had a likely lad of his own, a boy of nine in 1654, just the right age for the seven-year-old Countess Mary when the time came.

Tweeddale gave up his commission in September 1654 and was rewarded with a *douceur* of £2,647, which was exactly one year's interest (at 6%) on his debt to the Buccleuch estate, which now stood at £44,116 13s. 4d; in 1653 he had had to put the young countess in nominal possession of some of his lands as assurance that some payment on the interest would be regularly made. He would not be involved in the final stage of the negotiations for the reduction of the fine, which in the spring of 1655 was cut to £6,000 sterling, 40% of the original levy. This was a substantial saving in terms of money, but as a percentage it was not particularly generous. Most of the other fines were reduced to 25%; others, like that of Lady Wemyss' brother Rothes, to 33%; still others were suspended altogether—all three of the Scott tutors were thus fortunate. The £6,000 was promptly paid. The tutors, under old Harden's direction, were still doing an excellent job of managing. Even with all the taxes and expenses and fines—and uncollected debts like Tweeddale's—they still accumulated enough surplus over the seven years between 1651 and 1657 to lend out £120,000 on surety.

The payment to Tweeddale irritated Haychesters, who regarded it as tantamount to approval of Tweeddale's conduct in London. He complained that he had received no payment—he had, in fact, received £780 in expense money—and demanded that the other tutors formally approve his conduct, which they did, scribbling their approbation across the bottom of the document containing his formal request. What the payment to Tweeddale showed was that he had friends among the tutors, particularly Clerkington and Langshaw, the treasurer of the group. These two now effectively lobbied old Harden, the most influential member, in Tweeddale's favour. Lady Wemyss was thoroughly alarmed. She sent her husband south with a petition to Cromwell, asking the Protector to support her request to the tutors that she be allowed to continue to bring up her 'tender and weakly children' until they reached the age of eleven or twelve, 'the eldest being already going on eight'. The tutors had hitherto supported her, but at their last meeting Tweeddale had made a 'strong endeavor' to 'remove them [the children] forthwith from her for the future . . . for certain ends of his own'. Lady Wemyss had a right to be concerned: under Scottish law a widowed mother's right to custody expired when a child turned seven, as Mary did in September 1654. Her control of Anna would not expire until 1658, of course, but Anna hardly counted at this point. To Lady Wemyss' relief Cromwell sent a favourable reply to her request in November 1654. Her ladyship's wishes seemed 'very reasonable', he wrote, and he recommended that the tutors accede to them.

Lady Wemyss could not act on this document at once. In January 1655 she had to preside over the marriage of her daughter by her first husband, and in March she gave birth to her ninth child, her second by Wemyss. On June 6, however, she appeared at a meeting of the tutors to press her case. The tutors also had before them a letter from Tweeddale, whom they had invited to attend the meeting. He declined in chilling terms. 'Knowing how little my presence with you at this time could signify to the settling of the abode of the Countess of Buccleuch, or the good of any [of] the affairs of that family,' he wrote, 'I choose not to occasion unprofitable debate, being resolved to submit in my judgment to wiser, and in my will to higher powers'—an ambiguous phrase. The tutors were uneasy. Tweeddale was a man who stood well with the English. It had been rumoured that he would be chosen as a member of Monck's council. That did not happen, but in 1656 he was elected to the Protector's parliament, one of fourteen Scots chosen for the thirty Scottish seats, and he was appointed to a commission to try anyone accused of treason against Cromwell. It would not do to alienate him altogether. So the tutors temporised. They did not approve what would have amounted to a four-year grant of custody to Lady Wemyss, but instead of renewing her authority for one year only, as had been their practice hitherto, they granted it for two years, until Countess Mary, now almost eight, should turn ten, and they increased Lady Wemyss' expense money. Haychesters, of course, blamed this less-than-satisfactory result on the machinations of the endlessly evil Tweeddale.

Until this time the tutors had usually acted as a unit, held together by the influence and authority of old Harden. But at the end of 1655 he died, and the remaining nine instantly split into two groups and began to bicker with each other. The five south-country tutors, Harden's three sons including Haychesters, Gilbert Elliott of Stobs, and John Scott of Gorrenberry, a bastard son of old Earl Walter, suspected the four Lothian tutors, Scotstarvit, Clerkington, Langshaw, and Lawrence Scott of Bavielaw, of financial hanky-panky: they controlled the charter chest and the accounts. They had all, Haychesters observed, 'infeft their children in their estates, whereby they were not so responsible for their malversation as the rest of the tutors, of whom none then had done the like'. The south-country five could not act by themselves, however. By the terms of Earl Francis's will Clerkington and Scotstarvit had to be present: they, with the dead Harden, were the tutors *sine qua non*. Nor could the four Lothian tutors act by themselves, since the quorum was five. It was a formula for deadlock.

Haychesters now decided on a bold stroke. In 1655 the custody of the two precious children had been settled until 1657; there was no need to raise the matter in the tutors' meetings in 1656. So on August 13 of that year Haychesters and the other south-country tutors produced Lady Wemyss at the tutors' scheduled meeting to renew her demand for custody of the little girls until they each turned twelve, the age at which a girl could be legally married. The Lothian group was taken by surprise, and acquiesced. Lady Wemyss was less than two months out of childbed, which may well have contributed to the surprise. The tutors really had little choice, save to delay a decision until the following year, and they could hardly tell the forceful Margaret Leslie to her face that they thought she was being in any way inadequate as a mother. She was grateful to Haychesters. He was one step nearer his goal—but not yet there.

Haychesters' path became smoother still with the death of Clerkington, the most prominent member of the Lothian group, at the end of 1656. This tilted the balance in favour of the south-country group, and led to an arrangement whereby the younger Harden, who was Haychesters' brother, and Scotstarvit shared custody of the charter chest. It also led to a claim by Scotstarvit, the only remaining tutor *sine qua non*, to veto power over the actions of the tutors.* John Gilmour and the other lawyers whom the tutors consulted rejected this, so Scotstarvit boycotted the meetings of the tutors for a while, in spite of a conciliatory letter from Lady Wemyss. The latter, in notifying Haychesters of all this, adjured him to ask a friend of his who was going to London 'to have an eye on Tweeddale [now an M.P.] and his doings, for he is not idle to our hurt if he have power'. Scotstarvit eventually resumed his attendance at the tutors' meetings, full of complaint at the behaviour of the Harden group, who, he wrote to Lady Wemyss, 'have concluded amongst themselves to engross her Ladyship's estate to themselves and friends without me'. None of this would have happened, he said, if Lady Wemyss had had the good sense to support his claim to veto power.

The return of Scotstarvit boded no good to Haychesters and his plans. In 1657 Tweeddale launched yet another effort to lay hands on the estate by forcing his son on Countess Mary as a husband. He had allies among the Edinburgh legal and judicial fraternity. Lady Wemyss' own legal adviser, John Gilmour, was his friend. He had far more influence in English ruling circles than anyone Haychesters

---

* This claim was not as arrogant and far-fetched as it might seem. Earl Francis's will had made his wife sole tutor *sine qua non* (though without explicit veto power) as long as she did not remarry. In 1666 Leoline Jenkins, in an opinion on the claims of Countess Mary's executors, the earls of Rothes and Wemyss, argued that her grant to them of Tweeddale's debt was invalid because Scotstarvit in his capacity as the only remaining tutor *sine qua non* had not authorised it. See below, p. 51, footnote.

could count upon. He was very friendly with the Protector's good friend General John Lambert, with whom he was closely associated in parliament. More alarming still, Tweeddale began to cultivate the tutors. Not all of them were enchanted by Haychesters' influence with Lady Wemyss; they knew where it was tending. They had candidates of their own for Mary's hand, as the months wore on and her twelfth birthday approached. Gorrenberry had a son; Scotstarvit, a son or a grandson. Other names were floated: the earl of Lothian's son, or one of Eglinton's unmarried sons or his grandson, who took himself out of the running by eloping with the daughter of the impoverished earl of Dumfries. Rothes talked of a member of the Howard family, probably his mistress's brother. If we can believe the earl of Wemyss, Tweeddale even approached *him*, and offered to let him 'cut and carve' in the estate if he helped to bring about the longed-for marriage between Mary and the young Lord Yester.

By the end of 1658 Haychesters and Lady Wemyss were close to panic. The great Oliver had died, and the political kaleidoscope was shifting. The new Lord Protector, Richard Cromwell, was an unknown quantity; it was far from improbable that Tweeddale's friend Lambert would emerge as the strong man of the new regime. Mary was still under age, and she was not well. In answer to a solicitous letter from Lady Tweeddale, Lady Wemyss wrote on December 11, 1658 that the girls were both well, though Mary's arm was still troubling her. It had had five sores on it, but now there was only one. But under age or not, well or not, she was going to be married. One might suspect, indeed, that she was going to be married *because* she was unwell; if she died a spinster, Anna would inherit, and she was not yet eight. Tweeddale would have four more years in which to weave his plots. And die she might: in that same month of December 1658 Lady Wemyss collected £2,400 reimbursement for Mary's doctors' bills. She had been 'often subject to sickness some years past, and having a running sore in her arm yet under cure'. Haychesters could count absolutely on only two of the tutors now, his brother Harden and Elliott of Stobs; the others, he later wrote, were all lackeys and mercenaries. Even his other brother, Patrick Scott of Thirlestane, was ratting to Tweeddale, because, Haychesters wrote, he had played fast and loose with some of the Buccleuch rentals and hoped, if Tweeddale prevailed, to be spared an audit. Haychesters concluded that if he did not act now, his 'proper and lively boy' might never become earl of Buccleuch. There was no time to lose.

3

Marrying in Haste

Aristocratic marriages in seventeenth-century Scotland were not hole-in-corner affairs. Nor were they hastily concluded—muckle-mouth Meg (who, had she existed, would have been Haychesters's mother) and her drumhead contract were myths. Negotiating satisfactory terms for such marriages often involved considerable bargaining and could take quite a lot of time. There were three principal items to work out: the size of the bride's tocher, or dowry; the size of the conjunct fee, or jointure, the land that the groom's family turned over to the newlyweds, with the stipulation that the bride would enjoy the use of and income from that land during her widowhood if she outlived her husband, whether or not she remarried;* and the provision for the dowries of any daughters born of the marriage. The bargaining centred on the relationship between the size of the dowry and the amount of income from the jointure, and on the amount of the set-aside for the couple's daughters. As for the first of these: when Lord Balgonie, Lady Wemyss's son by her first husband, married the daughter of the earl of Carlisle in 1656, the girl's dowry, 45,000 merks, was five times the size of the jointure. The amount of a daughter's set-aside could be altered when the girl married. For example, Lady Jean Scott, as second daughter of the first earl of Buccleuch, was entitled to a dowry of 20,000 merks under the terms of her father's marriage contract. When she married the future earl of Tweeddale in 1644 she received

---

* These arrangements could sometimes beggar an heir. In 1670 William Baillie of Lamington appealed to the Scottish privy council for relief. His grandmother had the right to land with an income of 10,000 merks, and his mother to land worth 5,000; he had only 4,000 merks' worth for himself. The council was sympathetic and ordered his grandmother to turn over the family coal mines to Baillie (with the proviso that he supply her with coal for her house), and fifteen chalders of victual. (Rents were frequently paid in kind in Scotland, and measured in chalders of grain: a chalder equals 96 bushels.) The old lady balked, and got the victual allotment reduced to ten chalders.

40,000, as has been said, in return for renouncing any claim she might have to the estates of her deceased parents and siblings.

The contrast between normal practice and what happened at Wemyss Castle in the first weeks of 1659 is startling. On December 11, 1658, Lady Wemyss had written to her unloved sister-in-law Lady Tweeddale that it was too early to speak of Countess Mary's marriage. On January 1, 1659, she gave birth to her last child, a daughter, who one day would become countess of Wemyss in her own right. Early in that January Lord Wemyss, whom Haychesters disingenuously declared to be the real instigator of the marriage, wrote to Haychesters, asking him to bring his son to Wemyss Castle for a few days—as he was a student at St. Andrews, there was nothing remarkable in such a stopover. Mary took a liking to him—so Lady Wemyss and Haychesters said: it was because Mary wished it that the marriage was to take place as soon as possible. Her uncle Rothes looked the boy over, and approved. So, it goes without saying, did Lady Wemyss's son, Lord Balgonie, and her son-in-law, Lord Melville, who had married her daughter Catherine in 1655. The crucial question concerned the tutors; it was vital, in order to provide even a small shred of an appearance of legality, that five of them sign the marriage contract. Fortunately this was not difficult. Haychesters had two firm allies, Harden and Elliott, while Lady Wemyss could depend on Bavielaw and Langshaw. Bavielaw she employed as chamberlain of the rentals of Dalkeith and the coal at Sheriffhall. Langshaw, while not unfriendly to Tweeddale, was financially beholden to Lady Wemyss, as he was the general receiver of the rentals of the estate. So there was no need to approach the other three tutors, or to inform them of what was planned.

Now it was time to move, and it was an opportune time, since Tweeddale would be out of the country. He had been elected to Richard Cromwell's parliament, summoned for January 27. Early in February speed became more essential than ever, because Gorrenberry turned up unexpectedly, and most inopportunely, at Wemyss, bringing with him his own hopeful lad as a candidate for Mary's hand. He understood at once what was going on, and he would certainly notify Scotstarvit and Thirlestane at the very least, and probably Tweeddale as well.

There remained one final hurdle: the kirk. It was the rule that before any marriage could take place the banns had to be proclaimed on three successive Sundays, which meant a delay of three weeks.

But Haychesters and Lady Wemyss could not afford to wait three weeks, because the simple fact of the matter was that the marriage was illegal. Under the rules of both church and state no girl could marry until she was twelve years old, and Mary would not reach that ripe age until August 31, 1659. Church law did provide, however, that a presbytery had the power to dispense with the reading of the banns 'in some necessary exigents'; Haychesters and Lady Wemyss resolved to make use of this loophole if they could. On February 9 the earl of Wemyss and Gilbert Elliott asked the presbytery of Kirkcaldy to grant permission to the minister of Wemyss parish to perform the marriage at once. They cited the 'necessary exigents'—it would be interesting to know what they were, but the presbytery records do not say—and displayed the marriage contract. The presbytery unanimously, and quite improperly, granted the request. It had no right to endorse the marriage of an eleven-year-old, much less waive the usual rules in order to expedite such an impropriety. It should instead have prohibited the marriage and forbidden the reading of the banns.

The marriage contract presented to the presbytery was not the least remarkable aspect of this highly irregular business. Haychesters' son, young Walter Scott, aged fourteen (and therefore legally able to marry), brought nothing to the marriage but his own proper person. What he got was immense. Countess Mary agreed to take the legal steps necessary to create him earl of Buccleuch in name, and to grant him immediately a liferent—i.e., an annual income—out of the lands of the earldom in the amount of £24,000, about one fifth of the annual value of the estate. In the event that she predeceased him, a very likely possibility, the amount would be doubled. If she should die within a year and a day, and without issue—and clearly if she did so, there would be no issue—he was to have a lump sum of £120,000 in cash, the equivalent of a year's income from the estate, to be paid within three years. The reason for this provision was that under the law he would lose his claim to the liferent if she died that soon. Furthermore, if both she and Lady Anna died without heirs, the heirs to the entail, i.e. Jean Tweeddale and her son, would pay him annually an additional £18,666 13s. 4d. There were provisions for the daughters of the marriage, in the unlikely event that he and Mary had only girls, he predeceased her, and she had a son by a subsequent marriage.

These arrangements were extraordinarily one-sided. Everyone feared that Mary would soon die. Haychesters, blinded by ambition and greed, did not see the trap he was setting for himself. Lady Wemyss and her husband and brother were more clever: the patent illegality of the marriage would make the contract subject to legal challenge in the event of Mary's early death. They could thus avoid the pay-offs to her husband specified in it. In the meantime the prudent mother shored up her own financial position by means of a separate agreement, signed by all the parties to the contract, to the effect that the young couple would live with the earl and countess at Wemyss Castle for the next six years, until Mary turned eighteen. Lady Wemyss would collect £16,000 a year from the estate in expense money during that time, with an additional allotment of £3,000 a year for Anna. In addition Lady Wemyss pocketed £8,000 right away to pay for the expenses of arranging the contract and conducting the wedding. She must have turned a tidy profit on the latter: on the very evening of the day the presbytery of Kirkcaldy acquiesced in Lord Wemyss's request, February 9, 1659, the young couple were hustled down to Wemyss parish church and married by Henry Wilkie, its minister. Mary was eleven years, five months, and nine days old.

So far, so good. Six days after the marriage Lady Wemyss wrote to her legal adviser John Gilmour, saying that she expected Scotstarvit and Thirlestane to protest, but she was not especially worried. It would be pleasant to avoid the indignity of a public challenge, but indignity 'is all that I fear, for now I hope it [the marriage itself] is past all remedy'. She was soon undeceived. Tweeddale, joined by Scotstarvit, Thirlestane, and his kinsman the earl of Erroll, at once petitioned Monck, asking that both Mary and Anna be removed from Lady Wemyss's custody and sequestered on account of the irregular marriage, and shortly thereafter, with the additional support of Gorrenberry and the earls of Mar, Eglinton, and Roxburgh, they filed a statement with the commissary court at Edinburgh, which had the power to decide on the legality of marriages, asking that the marriage be annulled on the grounds that both Mary and her 'husband' were under age and that Mary had been improperly influenced by her mother, Haychesters, Harden, and Elliott; no mention was made of Bavielaw or Langshaw.

Tweeddale's petition was awkward for Monck. He felt that he could not order the sequestration of the little girls on his own authority, so on February 16 he referred the petition to the commissioners for the administration of justice, the Protectorate's replacement for the court of session, the monarchy's highest civil court. The commissioners acted promptly. On February 19, to Lady Wemyss's fury, they ordered Mary to be brought to Edinburgh at once and placed in the charge of the countess of Cassillis. They brushed aside Lady Wemyss's argument that the marriage was legal and was being challenged by malicious people out of disappointed ambition and rage—meaning Tweeddale. They then held a hearing on the petition for sequestration and interrogated the little girl. She declared that she had freely chosen to marry young Walter Scott. She also indicated 'the consummation of her marriage in the plainest possible language'. No doubt it was consummated—at least the opponents of the marriage never challenged Mary's statement and argued that she was still a virgin. Proof of her husband's age was exhibited. The commissioners were not persuaded that she was not being coached or coerced, however. Scotstarvit, who as the only remaining tutor *sine qua non* was the most appropriate petitioner to take the lead in the argument, declared that if Mary were once free of the 'sinister practices of her mother and tutors . . . she would quickly be sensible of the ruin and dishonor which they for their own ends have precipitated her unto'. He proposed either Lady Cassillis or the dowager countess of Mar, Mary's great-aunt, as an appropriate châtelaine. Lady Wemyss and her allies had protested vehemently against Lady Cassillis on the ground that she was a friend of Tweeddale's; so the commissioners offered Lady Wemyss a list of five, from which she could choose one: Lady Mar, Lady Alexander, the widowed daughter-in-law of Charles I's secretary of state, described by Haychesters as an 'old indigent lady' who was a friend of the treacherous Langshaw, and three kinswomen of the marquis of Argyll: his sister, his sister-in-law, and his daughter-in-law. This was a sinister and unexpected development, welcome to neither of the parties to the dispute. It was immediately suspected that Argyll wanted Mary for his second son, Neil Campbell, who was in his late twenties and still unmarried. None of the five was acceptable to Lady Wemyss, who thought of a brilliant counterstroke. Let Mary be sent to Dalkeith and put in the charge of General Monck and his wife. Who could object to that? And, after all, Dalkeith was Mary's house, even if the English authorities had been using it as their headquarters for the past seven years.

So Dalkeith it was. On February 26, seventeen days after the marriage, the commissioners decreed that Mary should reside there under Monck's tutelage until she turned twelve, unless the marriage was pronounced legal before that date. Under the circumstances Lady Wemyss had done very well. Mary was indeed sequestered at Dalkeith, but only for a limited time, and only from her husband, and even then not entirely: he could visit her occasionally. She wrote him a series of touching little notes in her childish scrawl over the next seven months, assuring him that she loved him, that she was well, that she 'would not neglect [to write] so often were it not that you desire me to, for fear lest it trouble my arm'—that ulcerated arm that seemed to get no better, despite her bravery about it. 'I bless the Lord I am very well myself, and I hope my arm is mending,' she wrote on another occasion. Her doctors did not help. In June 1659 Lady Wemyss employed a new one, a Dr. Borthwick, who applied a plaster to the arm and gave strict orders that it should not be removed, no matter how painful it was. Mary tried to be brave, but her screams in the night awakened General Monck, who ordered the plaster to be removed at once and expressed his anger at such treatment. No more was heard of Dr. Borthwick. Haychesters subsequently described the episode as 'an attempt upon the lady's person' and, since he could hardly blame Tweeddale, hinted that the culprit was Rothes, with whom he had quarrelled by the time he put his version of events on paper.

Mary was a dutiful and obliging child. She wrote to her husband's parents, to Haychesters expressing her alarm at the prospect that the machinations of her enemies might cause her sister Anna to be removed from her mother's care. 'If my sister were taken from us, I do think she were lost, it would break her spirit.' The enemy, of course, was Tweeddale. When her aunt Lady Jean Tweeddale came to Dalkeith to see her in March, Mary gave her a cold reception. Lady Wemyss reported with satisfaction to Haychesters that the two 'were very sharp one to another'. One might suppose that the sharpness was mostly on Mary's part. Lady Wemyss taught both her daughters to regard the Tweeddales with fear and hatred, and she taught them well.

Lady Wemyss herself spent a good deal of time at Dalkeith in the spring and summer of 1659, so much time that at one stage Tweeddale and Scotstarvit drafted a petition complaining that the purpose of sequestering Mary was being frustrated because Lady Wemyss had virtually moved in at Dalkeith. The estate's expense accounts suggest that there was some truth in this—money was spent on such

things as a jaunt to Leith in Monck's company to look over the fortifications there. Lady Wemyss was cultivating the general, and to
good effect. As the political picture became murkier in the latter part
of 1659, Lady Wemyss, her husband, and her brother urged the general to declare for the restoration of the king. The observant and
knowledgeable cleric Robert Baillie described her as a spokesperson
for the Scottish aristocracy on this matter—she was, Baillie added,
'a witty, active woman'. According to a statement written by a
Frenchman in England after Monck was dead, Monck was alleged
to have said that she and her husband had persuaded him to restore
King Charles. Whatever the truth may be, it is safe to assume that
after the king's return Lady Wemyss took as much credit for that happy event as she could. It was necessary: Charles had no reason to love
her husband. Lord Wemyss had been the spokesman of the committee of estates in August 1650 when Charles was compelled to sign a
statement expressing his repentance, not only for his own sins, but
also for the misdeeds of his father and the idolatry of his mother. It
was one of the most humiliating episodes of that awful year that
made Charles so hostile to all things Scottish. Wemyss escaped Charles's blacklist after 1660, which he may have owed to his wife. He
was wise to make no attempt to get involved in politics again.

Once Mary was settled at Dalkeith, the political and legal
manoeuvring began. What Tweeddale and his allies wanted was
plain enough: that the commissary court in Edinburgh nullify
Mary's marriage on the straightforward grounds that she was under
age and had been improperly married into the family of one of the
tutors, that she be kept out of her mother's hands, and that Anna
be removed from her mother's care. Lady Wemyss had every reason
to fear the court's decision. The commissary was Sir John Nisbet
of Dirleton, who had acted for Tweeddale in the petition for sequestration and whose wife was a Hay, 'with whom he declared he would
have no peace if he did not favor my Lord Tweeddale'. So she and
Haychesters decided on an immediate appeal to the Lord Protector. Wemyss and Haychesters—only the latter seems to have made
the trip*—were commissioned in the name of both little girls to go
to London to ask Richard Cromwell to approve Mary's marriage

---

* Wemyss had another preoccupation in the spring and summer of 1659: the
remarriage of his only surviving child by his first wife, his daughter Jean, now
30, to the heir of the earldom of Sutherland. She lived a long and litigious life
and died at 85 in 1715.

and Anna's remaining under her mother's care, and not to allow the commissary court at Edinburgh to pronounce judgment. In the formal petition Haychesters carried to London Tweeddale was accused of all sorts of sinister designs on the two children, including 'rape, sale, seduction, or other his subtle [!] attempts'. He wanted the countess for his own son, and had repeatedly tried to persuade the late Protector to sign a warrant turning the girls over to him; it was these machinations which had caused the decision to go ahead with the marriage. The petition went on to argue that however technically deficient the marriage might be, it was valid before God, since it had been properly performed and consummated. Haychesters was adjured to spare no expense, and indeed he did not: the estate eventually paid him in excess of £29,000, which suggests that he must have engaged in a certain amount of bribery—the expenses of his and Tweeddale's mission in 1654 came to only £2,400. If bribery there was, it was futile: Richard referred the petition to a subcommittee of his council, along with one from Tweeddale's side declaring that Mary had made an unsuitable marriage and asking that Anna be removed from Lady Wemyss and delivered to the petitioning tutors, Scotstarvit, Gorrenberry, and Thirlestane.

While these appeals were being carried to London, the thrust and counter-thrust continued at home. At the end of March 1659 a suit was filed with the commissioners for the administration of justice in Countess Mary's name, the purpose of which was to get a judgment removing Scotstarvit, Gorrenberry, and Thirlestane as tutors, and Tweeddale and Erroll as overseers, because they opposed the marriage. Tweeddale and his allies replied by filing a suit charging the five tutors who supported the marriage with corruptly abusing their trust. Early in April Tweeddale's side suffered a setback. Scotstarvit, who was a resident of Fife—Tweeddale was not—appeared at the semi-annual meeting of the synod of Fife and asked it to censure the presbytery of Kirkcaldy for having authorised the marriage without the usual reading of the banns. Such a censure would have been very useful for their party in persuading the commissary court to invalidate the marriage, the legality of which was the real, if unspoken, issue before the synod. Scotstarvit's move had been anticipated, however; the earl of Wemyss, a far more powerful figure in Fife than Scotstarvit, and Elliott were there to defend their request to the presbytery. Scotstarvit bungled his case by attacking the countess's marriage into the house of Harden as shameful, whereas if she had married his son or grandson, 'there would have been no stain upon her'. Wemyss heatedly retorted that if Scotstarvit were not so old, he would call him out. The moderator, the distinguished minister Robert Blair, told them both to be quiet. When Blair put the question to a vote, the synod, with nineteen dissenting, exonerated the presbytery of Kirkcaldy, in spite of the patent impropriety of its behaviour. The pliancy of both the presbytery and the synod in following the wishes of two great Fife earls, Wemyss and Rothes, suggests that historians have exaggerated the courage and independence of the Scottish clergy.

Then, on April 20, 1659, it was Lady Wemyss's turn to suffer a setback. Commissary Nisbet ruled that Tweeddale and his allies had a valid case against the marriage on the ground that Mary was under age; they could now confidently expect to have the courts pronounce it void. Nisbet then promptly adjourned his court so as not to have to listen to any appeal. Lady Wemyss was furious. She wrote to Haychesters in London that 'if it be in our power, we ought to study to get him out of his place. He is a malicious knave'. This was her standard reaction to legal setbacks: get the judge dismissed. As we shall see, her attitude four years later was much the same.

Since she could not count on Nisbet's dismissal, however, it behooved Lady Wemyss to take countermeasures. She consulted the Lord Advocate, a distinguished lawyer, George Lockhart of Carnwath, who was doubtful about the legality of an appeal to the Protector against Nisbet's ruling, except perhaps on procedural grounds, since there was a remedy available under Scots law, before the commissioners for the administration of justice. The first step was to go back to the commissary court and underline the fact that the marriage had been consummated. In any case, time was on Lady Wemyss's side: if Mary could be kept under Monck's protection until she was twelve, then she could legally ratify the marriage. An appeal to the Protector might delay any further court action long enough for that to happen. A document was prepared for the Protector, full of the usual abuse of Tweeddale and also, now, of both Nisbet and Scotstarvit, who, after his performance at the synod of Fife, had moved up to a high place in Lady Wemyss's pantheon of villains. He had wanted to get himself declared sole tutor *sine qua non*, ran the document, so that 'he might betray the Countess to whom he pleased'. Mary's marriage was valid—the petitioners underlined the decision of the synod of Fife, while being discreetly vague as to why it was necessary to proceed without the usual reading of the banns. And Mary had been improperly sequestered: the judges in doing this had usurped an authority belonging only to the Protector and his council. It was a skilfully prepared appeal.

The document was never used. At the beginning of May, 1659, Richard Cromwell resigned. The Protectorate was finished, the Commonwealth restored, and the members of the Rump back in the chamber from which Richard's father had forcibly expelled them six years before. These events in effect destroyed the legal basis for government in Scotland. The political union with England imposed by the Protectorate dissolved, and the Rump did not restore it. Government officials, including judges, were the creatures of the Protectorate: their authority vanished. There was no more central court system in Scotland—no one to hear Mary's case, no one to follow up on Nisbet's decree. Only local authorities—justices of the peace and sheriff courts—remained, authorised temporarily by the Rump. The only actual authority left in Scotland was Monck, who was necessarily preoccupied with keeping the peace and preventing royalist risings. Under the circumstances there was only one thing for both sides to do: appeal to the Rump.

Tweeddale was already on his way to London when Richard resigned. His own finances were in rather shaky condition, and he had to borrow over £5,500 from an Edinburgh merchant to pay his legal and travelling expenses. But borrow it he did, and when he arrived in London he immediately petitioned the parliament. His principal purpose now was to keep Mary sequestered beyond her twelfth birthday. Her marriage was a scandal and an offence against God, he said, and the court had declared against it. She should be brought to London, and the Scottish judges' authority should be renewed so that they could make the definitive pronouncement that Nisbet's ruling had foreshadowed. Haychesters was not far behind with his own collection of documents, the basic thrust of which was that Mary should be allowed to live with her husband and Anna with her mother. The opposition was trying to get the commissary to try the marriage, and he was ready to do so, even though his commission had expired with the Rump's return and he knew it. Mary's petition also contained a formal challenge to Nisbet's right to sit in judgment on the ground that he had behaved improperly. The petition went on to declare that their enemies wanted Anna in their hands if Mary should miscarry, 'to dispose of her to the ruin of the estate and family to their own sinister ends'. In response to the argument that Mary was under age, one of Haychesters' position papers tentatively tried out the argument that the marriage was valid in canon law, which applied in the absence of a specific act of parliament. The resigned Protector, they said, had authorised his council to hear their appeal; that appeal now lay with parliament. Their great worry was that the Rump would renew the commissions of the sitting judges; if that happened, Rothes wrote to Haychesters, they would lose. The case, said the countess's petition, should be heard in England.

Lady Wemyss had no intention of making any concessions to Tweeddale and his allies. To blacken the earl's reputation, Haychesters was fed Wemyss's story of Tweeddale's offer to let him 'cut and carve' in the estate in return for his support, and the canard that Tweeddale was responsible for David Scott's death a decade before. Lady Wemyss felt that there was no point in offering a bribe to Nisbet, as Haychesters suggested, and anyway he was distracted because his wife was dying. When she finally did pass away, Lady Wemyss gloated: 'Commissary Nisbet's marriage, by the death of his wife, was dissolved that same week he promised to dissolve my daughter's, and he is like to lose his wits for sorrow'. It was, Haychesters observed, 'a remarkable providence'. When a possible compromise was floated in London by Argyll and the radical lawyer Archibald Johnston of Wariston, that Tweeddale's son might marry Anna, Lady Wemyss would not hear of it. 'Truly I do not see,' she wrote to Haychesters, 'wherein ye can make any form of agreement with him for what concerns my daughter. . . . And for her sister, I think Tweeddale's interest in her is none at all, nor never shall, so far as I can have power.' What that 'ungrateful, false man' ought to do was pay Mary the money he owed her. And, in August a formal demand was made on Tweeddale in Mary's name to that effect. This did not come at a good time for the earl, who by this time had returned to Scotland. He had at last reached a settlement over the division of the delinquent earl of Dunfermline's estates, but the income from his share brought in only half of what he needed to make the interest payments on what he owed to Countess Mary. He had no hope of recouping very much until his foster-mother, the old dowager countess of Dunfermline, should die, which did not happen until December 1659. So in the course of 1659 Tweeddale had to sell some of his own lands and mortgage others. Small wonder that his mouth watered at the prospect of laying hands on the Buccleuch fortune and cancelling the debt.

At last the day Lady Wemyss longed for arrived: August 31, 1659, Mary's twelfth birthday. She wasted no time. On September 2, at Leith, Mary and her young husband made a formal declaration before witnesses, including Monck, ratifying their marriage and having the ratification registered in all the appropriate court books, including that of the commissary. According to one account a justice of the peace at Leith performed a second marriage ceremony. Be that as it may, Mary's sequestration was over. There was no legal authority in Scotland that could order its continuation, and Monck, given his other preoccupations, was no doubt happy enough to be free of this responsibility. At least he made no attempt to keep the young couple from returning to Wemyss Castle, where, wrote Haychesters, they cohabited until her death. Almost her first act on returning to her mother's home was to authorise her father-in-law to present a new petition to parliament, or to whatever authority he should find standing in London, to keep her sister Anna out of Tweeddale's hands. Lady Wemyss's vigilance never ceased.

Anna's fate was important, because Mary's health, alas, did not improve. Lady Wemyss put a brave face on matters, but she changed doctors frequently, looking in vain for one who could effect a cure. On April 26, 1660, a new team of 'physicians and surgeons' described Mary's condition as an ulcerated bone in her left arm, stemming from the elbow; they called it a tumour. They prescribed bleeding, purging (rhubarb and senna), loch-leeches, and a plaster, as well as various drugs. Early in May Mary made her will, appointing Haychesters her executor, rewarding him with the proceeds of many of the debts owing to the estate, and bequeathing £12,000 to his daughter Margaret. Mary's husband was to be the beneficiary of two enormous mortgages, one in the amount of 100,000 merks, the legal limit allowed under the entail, the other of £84,000, the amount of the fine (plus expenses) levied on the estate in 1654–55, on the dubious ground that this was a debt owing by Earl Francis at his death, which could therefore be added to the 100,000-merk limit. All this, of course, in addition to the £48,000 to which he would be entitled under the marriage contract. In an attempt to purchase the acquiescence of Rothes and Wemyss in this act of pillage, they were allotted the principal of the two biggest debts owing to the estate, Tweeddale's

£44,000, and £28,000 owed by Scott of Clerkington, and Rothes was forgiven the £17,333 he had borrowed. If all this had been implemented, there would have been precious little left for Anna. It was a will made in expectation of imminent death: the child countess was dying.

By early June 1660 Mary was too weak to visit her mother-in-law, to whom she sent a miniature 'which I hope you will wear in remembrance of me'. She could not even write this letter: it is in another hand. But within a few days of the sending of that sad missive Mary's mother decided that she was well and strong enough to travel to London. Lady Wemyss, for reasons to be indicated shortly, urgently needed to go there; if she took her daughter, she could charge the expense of the trip to the estate. But there was another reason for taking Mary with her: in London there lay one last hope of a cure—a miracle cure. As Mary put it in one of her little notes to her husband, written from the capital, 'My arm looks very well. We think the virtue of his Majesty's touch is like to cause the fresh bone cast out the rotten'.

His Majesty! The king had come into his own again. From now on the Buccleuch heiresses, and all those who longed, in Wemyss's graphic words, to cut and carve in their estate, would be playing on an entirely different board, and with pieces whose value—save for that of the king—was unknown. Whatever some of that king's more enthusiastic followers may have thought, however, Charles II was no worker of miracles. The rotten bone did not heal. Mary had less than a year to live.

4

A Beginning and an End

Of all the groups that made up the society of Charles II's three kingdoms, none was happier to see him return than the Scottish aristocracy. Their attitude is well summed up by the historian David Stevenson at the end of his magisterial two volumes on the history of the Scottish revolution. 'Socially and politically,' he writes, 'the experience of 1637–51 inclined the upper ranks of society to reactionary conservatism. The nobility in particular concluded that resistance to the king and establishment of presbyterian church government were socially subversive and politically disastrous. Undermining the king undermined the nobility; presbyterianism threatened social hierarchy and deference.' And at the end there was forcible subjugation by England, leading to toadying to English authority on the spot and bootlicking in London, whether of Protector or parliament. The power to decide the fate of the Buccleuch inheritance after Earl Francis died lay in London, not with the Scottish courts, or even with Monck. Everyone knew this, which is why Tweeddale and Haychesters spent so much time there. They were not alone. Everyone in Scotland with something to ask of the government did the same.

Now, in the spring of 1660, the long dark night of the Scottish aristocracy was over. The king, their king—no one forgot that the Stewarts were Scots—was coming home. No one knew exactly what he would do, but no one doubted that his power would be restored, or that he would listen to his natural counsellors, his noblemen. The great question was, which noblemen? Who would have his ear? And what impact would his return have on the fate of the Buccleuch inheritance?

One man who had been giving these matters a good deal of thought was Lady Wemyss's brother, hitherto a minor player in the Buccleuch drama, but now about to assume a far more significant role. John Leslie, seventh earl of Rothes, was considerably younger than his sister. He was born in 1630, which made him the same age as the king. He was eleven when his father, a major leader of the Covenanting party along with Argyll, died; so the boy was entrusted to the care of John Lindsay, earl of Lindsay and soon to be earl of Crawford as well, a good presbyterian, a soldier, a Covenanter and a leading Engager, whose daughter he married in 1648. Rothes grew up without much formal education—he is certainly the worst speller ever to have held high government office—and with a taste for soldiering. In his later years, when in his cups, which was often enough, he would ramble on about his desire to cast off the burden of governing the 'cindum' (kingdom) and return to the life of a 'sodger'. The king knew him and liked him. He became colonel of a regiment in December 1650, carried the sword of state at Charles I's coronation at Scone in January 1651, and was in the invading army that met its fate at Worcester the following September. Cromwell's troopers captured him in the streets of the city. Charles did not care for many Scots, but he never entirely forgot those who had shared that doomed adventure with him.

The English did not regard young Rothes as a particularly important prisoner. Both the earl of Lauderdale, also captured at Worcester, and Rothes' father-in-law Crawford-Lindsay, scooped up in Monck's raid on Alyth, were consigned to English prisons and did not emerge until the spring of 1660. But Rothes was allowed to go to Scotland on business from time to time, and to live at Newcastle, where he subsisted mainly on handouts from his sister. Like many other Scottish nobles he was in continual financial difficulties. By the late 1650s he was back in Scotland for good, but not necessarily always at liberty. In January 1658 Cromwell ordered him to be locked up in Edinburgh Castle because he was paying the kind of attention to Viscount Morpeth's wife which prompted the outraged husband to call him out—Rothes was being a trifle premature in his adoption of the lifestyle of Restoration aristocrats. He emerged in December 1658, thanks to General Lambert, in time to take part in the complications attendant on his niece's irregular wedding.

While his niece Mary was living at Dalkeith, Rothes often accompanied Lady Wemyss on her visits there, and ingratiated himself with Monck—like his father, Rothes was affable, charming, very good company, and in private conversation very persuasive. In 1667, when his rivals were contriving his political demise, their greatest concern was to keep him away from court: if he got an audience with Charles, they feared that their months of work to undermine him would be undone. Rothes was also an iron-headed drinker who could remain upright when most others had slipped from their chairs, and, like his sovereign, a dedicated pursuer of women. When he was serving as royal commissioner in Scotland in the mid-1660s, he was once chided for his behaviour; he rejoined that as commissioner his duty was to represent the king's person. It is not known what Charles II thought of this remark, if it was ever reported to him. Charles did, on occasion, scold him for his drinking, but not for his womanising. In time Charles decided that Rothes was politically incompetent, and gave him a job where he could do no harm. But he was never cast aside altogether, and died a duke in 1681.

In October 1659, a month or so after Mary's departure from Dalkeith, the chain of events that led to the king's restoration began. As part of his preparations for his march into England, Monck summoned commissioners from the shires and burghs to meet with him in November; Rothes was among their number. In April 1660 Rothes presided over an *ad hoc* meeting of nobles, lairds, and burgesses which drew up a loyal address to the king, stressing their desire to be of service to him in whatever he might command them. Rothes determined to deliver this message himself, in person, and as soon as possible. Like many other Scotsmen, he took ship to Breda.

There is no reason to suppose that Charles was not glad to see Rothes—he was glad to see everybody in that delirious spring— and Rothes received his rewards. He was not given a major governmental job, nor did he expect one; there were others with a greater claim on the king's gratitude. He became Lord President of the Council when the council was reconstituted, which had not yet occurred. This was an honorific post which did not entail much work but which indicated that he stood well with the king. He also got something more, something that, he hoped, might help to repair his broken fortunes: the gift of the wardship and marriage of his two little nieces.

The question of this wardship was a vexed and complicated one. Wardship was an old feudal burden, stemming from the military obligation of a vassal to his lord, which neither a minor nor a female heir could perform. It was not at all clear that the crown had any such rights over the Buccleuch estates. Earl Francis had been given in wardship when he inherited, but he had sold the property on which the crown's claim was based. When he died the king was not in a position to make any awards to anyone, and so the question did not arise. After Mary's marriage in 1659 Scotstarvit, who had a tricky and devious legal mind, suggested to Monck that he should ask the Protector for a gift of the wardship, on the theory that the Protector had succeeded to the rights of the crown. Monck refused, but Haychesters had it in mind to ask Richard Cromwell to make the gift to a third party with whom Haychesters had made a bargain. Richard's resignation effectively foreclosed that possibility.

No one, of course, could challenge the king's right to make a gift of the wardship of heiresses who were minors—provided that the gift was his to give.* It was unlikely in 1660 that anyone would have the effrontery to challenge the grant he had made to Rothes, and in any case there was no court in Scotland to hear such a challenge: the legal system was still suspended. So, too, was the signet office, that branch of the Scottish legal machinery which had the authority to declare that Countess Mary was twelve years old, and so no longer in the stage of pupillarity, and therefore competent to appoint curators to advise her in the management of her property in place of the tutors named in her father's will. There was also the unsettled question of the legality of her marriage. Because of the absence of the signet office Mary could not ratify it after she turned twelve. Might Rothes, as royally-appointed guardian, be disposed to raise the question of its legality? Or, more realistically, expect to be paid off not to do so? Lady Wemyss was very alarmed at what Rothes had done when she learned about it from her husband, who, like everybody else of any importance in Scotland, had gone to London to seek the king's favour. Hitherto Lady Wemyss seems to have thought of Rothes as a wayward and not altogether responsible kid brother—in May 1660, when Rothes was in London on his way to Breda, she wrote to Lauderdale asking him to protect Rothes from Morpeth and his brothers, but not to tell him that she had asked. Now, her attitude abruptly changed. Rothes was clearly not a kid brother any more. He was up to something, which would probably be expensive. It was imperative to get to London at once.

So in June 1660 Lady Wemyss and her ailing daughter hastened to the capital. Rothes was most obliging. Perhaps he showed his sister the draft of a document he had drawn up discussing the grounds

---

* In 1660 the English parliament ended the crown's right of wardship. No such formal abolition took place in Scotland until 1747.

on which he expected to be compensated because he was not a dona-
tor in Mary's marriage contract, which had been executed before
he became her guardian! This was legally very dubious. So Rothes
acquiesced in his sister's wish that the gift of ward and marriage be
altered to make Wemyss joint guardian with him. What Rothes
had done was to send Lord and Lady Wemyss a signal. He intended
to be cut in, and his good standing with the king made it impossible
for them to ignore him. Lady Wemyss was not altogether happy,
and from this time forward she never really trusted him. But there
was nothing to be gained, at this point, from quarrelling with him.
Furthermore, he had some useful advice—at least Haychesters
thought that the plot originated with him. If Mary should die, there
was no reason why anything should go to her husband. As a first step
in that direction, they should all work to be sure that he had no support in London—meaning Monck, his only possible major ally.
There was no need to worry about Tweeddale: it was as much in
his interest as in theirs that Haychesters and his son be left out in
the cold.

So, when Haychesters and his lively boy arrived in London later
that summer, they met with a series of nasty surprises. Monck was
very chilly, thanks, Haychesters thought, to Lady Wemyss. Worse
still, the king created the young man, not earl of Buccleuch, as they
had confidently expected, but earl of Tarras, a title taken from their
own estates, not Buccleuch's, and the grant of the earldom was only
for life. Haychesters' own knighthood was a mean consolation.
What in the world had happened?

Haychesters had no trouble leaping to a conclusion. The villain
was Rothes, who now took his place as a Wicked Uncle almost on
a level with Tweeddale. And, in fact, Haychesters decided, he and
Tweeddale were working together to invalidate Mary's marriage.
Rothes won over one of the tutors, Scott of Langshaw, who henceforth followed him 'in his designs on the family of Buccleuch, which
had raised him [Langshaw] from the dunghill'.* In early 1660 Rothes
and Tweeddale worked it out that Rothes would back Monck, and

* Haychesters' gibbering hatred of all those who had a part in frustrating him is
shown by his treatment of Langshaw in his 'Information'. In 1655 and 1656
Langshaw was secretly working for Tweeddale; by 1660 he was Rothes'
creature. In actuality Langshaw, who was a notary and the family's general
factotum, seems to have been a man of independent judgment, concerned to do
what was best for the estate.

Tweeddale his opponent Lambert, so that one of them would be the victor's friend. Each of them slandered Haychesters to his patron. Rothes' purpose in asking for the wardship was to sell Anna to Tweeddale for his son. He and Tweeddale, in collaboration with Secretary of State Lauderdale, filled offices in Scotland with men who would be beholden to them, like Sir John Gilmour, who became president of the court of session. This unholy alliance, these two wicked uncles, working hand in glove, combined to destroy the prospects of the new earl of Tarras and his deserving father—so wrote the newly minted knight bitterly, some years after the fact.

Virtually all of this was pure fantasy. The only accurate assumption Haychesters made was that neither Rothes nor Tweeddale had any interest in his welfare or that of his son. Otherwise their interests were directly opposed. If Rothes was to have a cut of the pie, his sister had to be in charge, or else the wardship ploy had to work to Rothes' advantage. Tweeddale's whole purpose was to oust Lady Wemyss and get control of the girls himself. Rothes knew this perfectly well. Far from collaborating with Tweeddale in the spring of 1660, he was doing his best to rouse suspicion and mistrust of him in the circles around the king. In April 1660 Rothes wrote to Lauderdale that Tweeddale was spreading lies about Lauderdale's behaviour. He was a dangerous man: 'really I believe that he will prove to those that trusts [*sic*] him another Argyll'. And as for collaboration on patronage: Tweeddale's principal ally among the tutors, Scotstarvit, was ousted from his position in the government and fined £6,000. Scotstarvit and Tweeddale's two other allies among the tutors rather imprudently petitioned Charles not to be held responsible for whatever Lord and Lady Wemyss might do about Anna, given their illegal behaviour respecting Mary. As for Tweeddale himself, he made the ritual pilgrimage to London and was well enough received. He got the form of his land tenure changed so that it would not be subject to wardship in future, and he was made a privy councillor. But it cannot be said that Charles ever fully trusted him, now or at any time in the future, even in the days of his greatest influence. Like the earl of Shaftesbury in England, he had once been a servant of Cromwell. Charles was prepared to use such men, and to reward them, but never to give them his confidence, and to cast them aside if they ceased to be useful. Both men suffered this fate at about the same time, in the early 1670s. The ambitious Shaftesbury went into opposition; the more philosophical, or more pliant, Tweeddale went home to Yester House.

In September 1660 Lady Wemyss, her mission in London accomplished, returned home with her husband and daughter. So too did Rothes. The trip had done Mary no good. The king's touch had not cured 'the cruells in her arm', as the diarist John Lamont described her ailment; shortly after her return she fell ill of the measles, and then came down with a fever. Winter came, and no recovery. Her mother, her stepfather, and her solicitous uncle Rothes gathered round. Amenable as ever, the child put her hand to a new will drafted by their lawyers. Her beloved husband and his grasping father were entirely cut out. Haychesters was no longer executor; his daughter got no bequest; there were no huge mortgages in Tarras's favour. Instead Rothes and Wemyss were named co-executors, with the right to pocket all the income from rentals and debts owing to the countess at the time of her decease, plus the principal owing on three specific debts: that of Rothes himself, and those of Haychesters and John Scott of Newburgh, for which Harden was cautioner. There was only one bequest, of £10,000 to Mary's cousin Lady Mȧry Montgomery, which took the form of authorising a debt owing to the Buccleuch estate by her father, the new earl of Eglinton, to be paid to Lady Mary. When the estate was inventoried after Countess Mary's death, the net value of the debts and goods to which the executors were entitled, after deduction for such expenses as the cost of her funeral, was over £96,000, half for each. The inventory also demonstrated how well the tutors had done for themselves over the years. Of the eight left alive in 1661, six owed money, either because they had borrowed it, like Haychesters, or because they were chamberlains or lessees. Many other members of the Scott family also shared in the good things. Of the tutors, only Scotstarvit and Elliott, the one tutor who was not a Scott, were excluded, which may well explain Scotstarvit's bitterness toward Lady Wemyss.

Mary's will was an extraordinary document. Tarras and Haychesters were at Wemyss at the time, but they knew nothing about it. Lady Wemyss kept them out of the sickroom as much as she could, and was, Haychesters later wrote, 'ever devising quarrels with them, and suggesting harsh things of them, to the innocent dying lady, to justify the unhandsomeness of the posterior testament'. The executors were so grasping that they opened themselves to a later legal challenge, especially Rothes, whose 'loan' of £12,000 contracted the previous December, would now be forgiven—the first fruit of his bold ploy over the wardship. By law executors were entitled to the movables and personal property of the deceased, what was called the executry. They were not entitled to rentals or interest on long-term debts like Tweeddale's, save enough to cover expenses, as long as there were outstanding debts; rentals had to be accounted for to the next heir. Mary's will, however, assigned Rothes and Wemyss 'debts, rents of all lands . . . and other rents or annualrents [interest income]'. The child was almost certainly unaware that she was robbing her sister. Rothes and Wemyss further reinsured themselves by getting Mary to sign a separate codicil guaranteeing them at least as much as they would have got under her will.

Anna, as heir-presumptive, was being pillaged on a massive scale.*

Little more than a month after signing this will in a pathetically shaky hand, Mary died, on March 12, 1661. Hers was a short and sad life. She suffered the common fate of child heiresses, to be fought over by greedy relatives who cared much more for her money than for her—Gloria Vanderbilt comes to mind. In Mary's case there was the further misfortune of the disease, probably bone cancer, that sent her to her early grave. What we know about her suggests that she was an amiable little girl who did what she was told by her formidable mother. It is easy to be too hard on Lady Wemyss. By 1661 she had already buried six children, half of those she had borne; before she died she would bury three more. She did not neglect Mary. She was constantly seeking for some way to make her well; hence the constant shifting of doctors and the last, unwise, trip to London to have her touched by the king. Among the debts owing by Countess Mary at her death were £1,113 18s. to an Edinburgh apothecary for drugs, and £480 'to Alexander Pennycuik, chirrurgian, foir imbalming the defunct her corpis, and for paines and medicamentis furnischit to hir the tyme of hir sicknes'. If Lady Wemyss can be legitimately blamed, it was for paying too much attention to the insinuations of the ambitious and greedy Haychesters, and allowing him to talk her into consenting to the premature marriage. She was right to be suspicious of Tweeddale. But

---

* In 1664, after Anna's marriage to the duke of Monmouth, their curators raised the issue of the long-term debts before the court of session. Rothes and Wemyss submitted all their claims to Charles's judgment; in 1666 the king ruled that they were not entitled to four long-term debts, including Tweeddale's, but they got virtually everything else Mary had bequeathed to them. This ruling was so favourable that in the 1690s Anna sued their heirs on the ground that they had induced Mary to sign a will that allowed them to profit illegally.

the remedy she chose to counter his plots, if plots there were—the evidence is murky—was far from wise.

With Mary's death the roof fell in on the bereaved widower and his father. The new countess of Buccleuch, little Anna, was only ten; therefore the tutors recovered their authority, which they would possess, under Earl Francis's will, until she turned twelve. Lady Wemyss now turned to the formerly despised Scotstarvit. She needed him because the tack that she now wished to take was to concede that he had been right all along: the marriage, and its expensive contract, which provided young Tarras with an income of £48,000 a year for life, were invalid. A meeting was held at Wemyss's lodgings in Edinburgh, where he was staying because the Scottish parliament was in session. Lady Wemyss's two followers amongst the tutors, Langshaw and Bavielaw, met with the three original opponents of the marriage, Scotstarvit, Gorrenberry, and Thirlestane. They agreed that they would manage Countess Anna's affairs to the exclusion of the other three, and that they would ask the court of session to invalidate Mary's marriage contract on the grounds on which Tweeddale had originally protested against it: Mary was under age when she signed it, and the contract was grossly inequitable. They also agreed, at Scotstarvit's insistence, to include among their arguments the fact that he, as sole remaining tutor *sine qua non*, had never consented to the marriage.

What could Haychesters do? He apparently had no friends left anywhere. About the only bargaining chip he still had, apart from the contract itself, was the fact that his brother and ally Harden still held one of the keys to the charter chest. The other five demanded its surrender. He, Harden, and Elliott, 'the only three tutors who are not of a mercenary nor sordid condition', took legal advice. The lawyers had nothing better to suggest than an appeal to the royal commissioner, the earl of Middleton, and the executive committee of the parliament, the committee known as the lords of the articles, since the court of session had not yet been reconstituted. They did appeal to the committee; the other five tutors filed a counter-statement announcing their intention to sue the three for misconduct in office. The lords of the articles in effect sided with the majority; on May 31, 1661, they ordered that the whole business be referred to the court of session. Haychesters did the best he could by taking the offensive. He initiated a legal process to require the five tutors to admit him and his allies to their meetings. The five flatly refused, unless

the three, and Tarras, renounced all benefit from the marriage contract and agreed to stand trial on charges of mishandling the affairs
of the estate. This was in January 1662. The five felt very confident. The reconstituted court of session, presided over by Lady Wemyss's former legal adviser Sir John Gilmour, was undoubtedly
going to support them. Haychesters thought so too. In October
1661 he and Tarras were prepared to settle for 20,000 merks a year,
less than one third of what Tarras was entitled to under the contract. When the court of session summoned Haychesters to respond
to the attacks on the contract, he offered to submit the whole matter
to the king for judgment, and 'with some importunity' asked that
his statement be read. The court refused, and ordered him to produce
the contract itself. He avoided doing so by simply failing to appear.
He knew that this would mean a negative verdict, but at least no judgment on the merits of the contract itself would have been pronounced. Lady Wemyss and her allies were satisfied. They did not
pursue the action for mishandling of funds, though it was never formally dropped. Lady Wemyss was not, in fact, too eager to have such
a charge pursued, since it would involve close inspection of how
the rental income of the last two years of Mary's life had been spent.

Haychesters allowed the case against the contract to go by default
because he hoped that at some future time there might be some hope
of salvaging something. For the present, however, things looked
bleak. He and his brother Harden were among those fined by parliament in 1662, along with Scotstarvit, for their conduct during the
interregnum. Late in that year he proposed to Lady Wemyss that Tarras might surrender his claims to Anna's prospective husband in return for compensation; Lady Wemyss ignored him. He twice tried
a direct appeal to the king, in 1663 and 1664, but by then Charles
had a direct interest in preserving the assets of the Buccleuch estate
for its holders, and the petitions got nowhere. Charles had been carefully informed about the nature of the contract and the grounds on
which the five tutors had sued for its nullification. So when Haychesters presented his petitions, Charles simply handed them to Secretary Lauderdale, who dealt with them. The second one, in fact,
was turned over to Tweeddale, who must have relished the assign-
ment, to draft a reply. When it came, from the hand of Tweeddale's
legal adviser Sir John Nisbet, it was to the effect that nothing be
done until Anna's husband's curators were named, which, wrote
Haychesters, caused him to come home, 'knowing very well what

sort of curators [her husband] would be furnished with'—and, indeed, they included Rothes, Tweeddale, and Lauderdale himself. After all, Anna's husband, the duke of Monmouth, was King Charles's eldest bastard, and the king doted on him. Small wonder that Haychesters' petitions got nowhere; small wonder that he gave up and went home. The one step he would not take—Lady Wemyss urged it on him for obvious reasons—was to make a formal legal submission of Tarras's claims to the king. He knew that the result would be a judgment which would mean that, as he later wrote Tarras, 'thereafter ye could have no further pretense in law'. As with the court of session, Haychesters judged that it was better to keep Tarras's slender chances alive than to run the risk of seeing them vanish forever.

In May 1671 Tarras himself, now a young man of twenty-five and just returned to Britain after some years spent on the continent, tried his own hand. There seemed to be only one reasonable chance: the duke and duchess of Monmouth themselves must become his advocates with the king. He went to see them, and they agreed to arrange for access to Charles so that Tarras could present a petition. But first Charles wanted to know what was going to be in it; so Monmouth asked. Tarras said that the marriage contract entitled him to £48,000 a year; he was now ten years in arrears; so he was going to ask for half the total as a lump sum—£240,000, or £20,000 sterling. Would you be satisfied with a pension instead? asked Monmouth. No, replied Tarras; pensions 'are ill-paid and uncertain', which was indeed the case in Restoration Britain. But the king did not have to pay him all at once, said Tarras; the payments could be spread out over four or five years, and perhaps he would agree to settle for a lesser sum. Tarras was asking for a lot. The petition was, nevertheless, duly presented to the king, Monmouth taking Tarras around to the house of Charles's mistress the duchess of Cleveland for the purpose. While he was waiting for a reply, Tarras importuned his former sister-in-law to speak to the king on his behalf; Anna promised that she would, but somehow she never found the opportunity. After two days in suspense Tarras went to see Monmouth again, and learned that Charles had referred the petition to Lauderdale. The following day Tarras called on Lauderdale, and encountered him just outside his lodgings. The secretary told him abruptly that he would get nothing. 'Nothing, my lord?' he asked. 'Nothing,' said Lauderdale. 'I am to tell the duke of Monmouth of it,' and turned on his heel. Tarras hung around London for a few more months, badgering Anna and Monmouth to do something for him. They tried—or so they said. Charles's response to their pleas was that he had made Tarras an earl, and that was enough. Tarras never saw a penny of the money. Like his father, he had doomed his chances by asking for too much.

Tarras, 'the mock Earl Tarras whom they say the Duchess calls brother', in Tweeddale's scornful phrase, lived for twenty-two years after this final rejection. Anna, who seems to have liked him—or perhaps felt a bit guilty about how he had been treated—employed him as an estate manager in the later 1670s, in return for a formal renunciation of his claims under the marriage contract, which he made in 1678. He was apparently involved in the Rye House Plot in some way, and in September 1684 found himself in Edinburgh Castle charged with treason. Anna's help, and a prompt confession which sent another man to the scaffold, saved his life. He died in 1693. The son of his second marriage, to the daughter of an East Lothian laird, inherited his estates though not his title.

So ends the sad tale of the child bride and groom, pawns in the hands of their elders, her mother and his father, two hard-nosed, calculating parents. Their marriage was a move in the parents' game, and they got precious little from it. Mary at least died young, but Tarras was haunted by might-have-beens for over thirty years. When the stakes are so high, the pawns matter little enough to those who manipulate them. The game was far from over, however. Even before Mary's death it had been resumed, on a different board, with different pawns, two major new players, and for much higher stakes. With Mary there was a huge fortune involved, but that was all. With Anna what came to be involved was not only the fortune but also the course of high politics and the destiny of kingdoms.

5

A Royal Bridegroom

M ary's death was not unexpected, and all the interested parties
had been making their preparations. The new will the dying
child had been persuaded to sign amply provided for her mother
and stepfather and her uncle Rothes. In 1661 Earl David, perhaps in
anticipation of the money he was to receive, began the construction
of a harbour 'by west Saltgreine' to facilitate the marketing of his coal
and salt, and rebuilt it after a devastating storm in 1662. Tweeddale
also was taking precautions. He and his three allies amongst the tutors, Scotstarvit, Thirlestane, and Gorrenberry, drew up a petition
to the king, which they may never have presented, arguing that there
should be no gift of Anna's wardship to anyone other than Anna herself, on the ground that any Buccleuch lands held of the king *cum maritagio* were inconsiderable. Tweeddale knew perfectly well that any
gift of her wardship would not be made to him, and could work only
to his disadvantage.

Tweeddale had heard rumours. On February 28, 1661, two weeks
before Mary's death, Rothes wrote what was, for him, a long letter
to Secretary Lauderdale, saying that Tweeddale had heard that
Rothes was to get the wardship of Lady Anna. Tweeddale, Rothes
went on, was planning to petition the king, either alone or in company with others, to prevent this. It was rumoured that Lauderdale
had made this suggestion to Tweeddale, which, Rothes said, he did
not believe. And with good reason, since Rothes had enlisted Lauderdale to help him do precisely what Tweeddale suspected him of
doing: getting Anna's wardship for himself.

Anna's destiny had been on Rothes' mind for some time. At the
time of Mary's marriage his father-in-law, the earl of Crawford,
pressed him to get Anna for his eldest son, Lord Parbroath, and
Rothes had promised that he would try to arrange this. He had dis-
cussed Anna's marriage with Lady Wemyss; there was some talk of
Eglinton's second son, who was their nephew. It seems likely that

Rothes did not much care who finally became Anna's husband, as long as he could make money out of the arrangements, and the surest way to do that was to become her sole guardian. Just when he approached Lauderdale is not known. But almost from the beginning of the restored regime there had been a working political alliance between the two. In November 1660 they had even arranged a kind of code. Lauderdale, as secretary of state, resided permanently at court. If Rothes, in passing on from Edinburgh a request to the king, wrote about it in his own hand, Lauderdale was to take it seriously. If he used one of his secretaries, Lauderdale could disregard it.

In short, Lauderdale found Rothes useful, and he was the king's friend. There was far more reason to accommodate him than Wemyss, the old Covenanter, whose behaviour Charles had found so offensive during his awful year in Scotland in 1650–51. So Lauderdale cooperated with Rothes, and got him what he wanted. On February 28 Rothes had cautioned him to say nothing until he had word of Mary's death: no one was to know what was afoot. When Mary died Rothes wrote to Lauderdale at once. He also wrote an egregiously hypocritical letter to all those in Scotland who might thwart him, including Wemyss, Tarras, Haychesters, and his sister's son Lord Balgonie, saying that he had sent the sad news to Lauderdale, 'with undeniable pressing reasons for a ratification of his Majesty's former gift of the ward of . . . lady Anna . . . in the same way as it was formerly', in order to nip in the bud the designs 'of those we apprehend to be our enemies'. This piece of chicanery may not even have been necessary. Lauderdale had done his job very well. On March 22, ten days after Mary's death, Charles made the gift of Anna's wardship and marriage to her loving uncle, and to him alone. Rothes was profuse in his thanks to his friend the secretary.

Lady Wemyss was caught completely by surprise. Her brother's underhandedness and treachery appalled her; his greed was apparently limitless. Her paranoia with respect to her former brother-in-law provided her with the obvious explanation: Rothes would use his power as guardian to sell Anna in marriage to the detested Tweeddale's brat. He and Tweeddale were being very friendly at the meeting of parliament, which was currently in session—neither she nor anyone else knew that Rothes was behaving this way at Lauderdale's request, for the secretary's own political purposes. Tweeddale's debt to the Buccleuch estate was growing—at Mary's death it stood at £52,027. He showed no signs of paying it, in spite of the recent improvement in his own financial circumstances owing to the death of his foster-mother, the old dowager countess of Dunfermline, which permitted him to take possession of more of the Dunfermline property. The situation looked very dangerous to Lady Wemyss.

It was, in fact, even more dangerous than she knew. Tweeddale had put a question to his lawyer-kinsman Sir John Nisbet which, if he had received a favourable answer that withstood legal challenge, would have meant immediate victory. Earl Francis in his will had used the following language: 'By a band of tailzie . . . we have entailed our estate to the heirs male whatsoever of our own body, which failing to our eldest heir female of our own body, without division, which failing to the other heirs of tailzie and provision mentioned in the said band'. The 'eldest heir female of our own body' was now dead. Did that mean, asked Tweeddale, that only Mary was included in the entail? And that now his wife, Lady Jean, was the rightful holder of the estate, cutting Anna out entirely? Nisbet's answer was emphatically in the negative, and the ploy was never tried. If Tweeddale had not kept a memorandum in his papers, we would not know that the question had ever been asked.

What could Lady Wemyss and her husband do about Rothes' treachery? Their first thought was to appeal to Monck, their most reliable, in fact their only, friend in Charles's entourage. Monck's reply was discouraging. He found it hard to believe that Rothes would 'do so unhandsome a thing', he wrote to Earl David on April 23, but the only remedy he could see was for Rothes himself to change his mind and ask that, as before, Wemyss be made joint guardian with him. Otherwise, said Monck, there was nothing to be done. The attitudes of the eight remaining tutors, now once more legally empowered to manage the affairs of an under-age countess, gave Lady Wemyss further cause for unease. She had begun the discussions over the reduction of Mary's marriage contract, which meant conciliating Tweeddale's three friends among the tutors, the men who had argued from the beginning that the contract was illegal, and holding onto her two steady supporters, Langshaw and Bavielaw. But were they indeed her steady supporters? If the bitter Haychesters is to be believed, Langshaw had transferred his allegiance to Rothes. And Tweeddale was working on Bavielaw: on May 1 he formally promised Bavielaw that if Lady Jean or her heir came into the estate, he would be held guiltless of all his acts as tutor, save for an accounting of the rents of Dalkeith for 1658 and 1659, the last years of the English occupation. If Tweeddale and Rothes were really in alliance, there might well be a majority of tutors who would approve the marriage of Anna to Tweeddale's heir.

So Lady Wemyss thought of a brilliant ploy, one that would cut through all the difficulties and solve all her problems at once. She would offer Anna as a bride to the king. Not to Charles himself, of course, though he was still unmarried at the age of thirty-one, but to his son, his eldest bastard, James Croft, as he was called, a lad two years older than Anna. The fact of his bastardy, which would have proved an insuperable obstacle in an aristocrat's son for such a catch as Anna, was no problem when an illegitimate royal child was in question. No matter that Lady Wemyss had no legal authority to offer Anna's hand to anyone: neither her brother nor the tutors would dare even to hint at an objection if the king accepted the proposal. Undoubtedly (though we have no record) Earl David approved. As for Anna, she was only ten. What opinion could she possibly have, other than her mother's?

On May 28, 1661, Lady Wemyss made the offer to the king. Her letter has not survived, but Charles's response, dated June 14, has. It was a delighted acceptance. Anna was as rich a prize as he could want for his boy. Lady Wemyss was ecstatic. 'Your Majesty's most gracious letter,' she wrote in reply, made her 'more happy than anything else in the world could have made me.' Small wonder: she would now be connected with royalty. The hated Tweeddale would be foiled. There would now be no trouble about the reduction of Mary's marriage contract, or with the tutors, who all promptly fell into line. The five who supported the reduction wrote to Rothes, explaining that Lady Wemyss had no authority to offer Anna's hand, but that they, who did have the authority, would be happy to oblige the king if he would get in touch with them. It is not known if Charles paid any attention to this piece of officiousness. Haychesters and his two allies among the tutors realised that, whatever the legal merits of Mary's marriage contract might be, it would be political suicide to attempt to uphold it now. Haychesters' and Tarras' only hope was to be publicly enthusiastic about the proposed marriage and butter up Lady Wemyss in the hope that she might have some crumbs for them, which she occasionally showed signs of being willing to bestow. So Haychesters actually went to London with an address to the king in support of the proposed marriage, which would dash 'the hopes of any who have hitherto or may hereafter attempt any-thing to the dishonor or prejudice of that lady or the dissolution or embezzling her estate', a rather long list in Haychesters' mind by now. If for whatever reason the marriage did not take place, the king was urged to be sure that the five tutors who had usurped the admin-istration of Anna's estate did nothing dishonourable. There is no evi-dence that Charles ever saw this document.

Lady Wemyss suffered only one disappointment. Charles would not alter the grant he had made to Rothes. 'I am confident,' he wrote blandly to her, 'you will not mislike it, when you consider it is for the advantage of the family you are come of, and for a person I have so great kindness for.' Charles had ordered Rothes to give him the necessary assurances in writing, and he had complied: 'I shall not meddle as to the disposal of my niece without your Majesty's com-mands'.* Lady Wemyss knew what Charles's letter meant: Rothes would have to be paid off in return for his formal consent to the mar-riage. She was not pleased, and her relations with her brother re-mained stormy for some time.

Lady Wemyss's move was so brilliant that contemporaries were unwilling to believe that it had been her idea. The earl of Clarendon thought that Lauderdale was the chief promoter of the match. Sir George Mackenzie, the lawyer and judge, gave the credit to Rothes. The unspoken assumption was that a mere woman could not possibly have contrived such a spectacular ploy—though Mack-enzie himself described Lady Wemyss as 'a person of much wit and subtlety'. It is clear from the evidence that neither Rothes nor Lauder-dale was the initiator of the match, and there is no reason to doubt that Lady Wemyss was. She had repeatedly shown her ability to get what she wanted, and the woman who thought up the manoeuvre of entrusting Mary to General Monck when she was in a very tight corner in 1659 was perfectly capable of hitting on the idea of offering Anna to the king.

* Just when Rothes learned of his sister's plans for Anna is uncertain. Charles's letter to Lady Wemyss about the wardship is dated August 25, 1661. Rothes' to Charles is dated 'the 13th', without month or year; it was probably written in August. A letter Rothes wrote to Lauderdale thanking him for securing the wardship is dated 'Oct. 13', perhaps a slip of the pen for August, or, more likely, September. The interesting thing about the letter is that Rothes asks Lauderdale who is to marry Anna; he hopes that Lauderdale can tell him, 'if you be not tied by command'. If the date October 13 is correct, it indicates that Rothes was in the dark four months after Charles accepted Lady Wemyss's offer.

Thus King Charles became personally involved in the destiny of the family of Buccleuch and its immense fortune. As the prospective father-in-law of the young heiress he paid close attention to the business of the estate, always with the interest of his beloved son in mind. Charles II is one of the most enigmatic men ever to have worn the crowns of his three kingdoms. The longer one studies his career, and the more detail one absorbs, the greater the puzzlement becomes. All sorts of assessments have been made of him; perhaps the oddest is that of William III's physician James Wellwood, who described Charles as Tiberius without his vices—and he meant it as a compliment. Charles's most recent scholarly biographers, John Miller and Ronald Hutton, in effect throw up their hands. To Miller Charles had the mentality of the returned émigré, always fearful of a new upheaval. He was mistrustful and duplicitous, and habitually dissimulated. 'No one will ever be entirely sure about his motives and intentions,' Miller writes. 'Probably he was not sure himself.' Hutton entitles his summation *Monarch in a Masquerade*. 'Behind those coverings,' runs his final sentence, 'something was always missing.'

Lacey Baldwin Smith, in his study *Henry VIII: the Mask of Royalty*, has taught us that monarchy is often a matter of the wearing of masks. In the case of Charles II the masks were the result of his *annus horribilis* in Scotland in 1650–51. The hopeful and inexperienced youth of twenty who set out to take vengeance on his father's murderers and resume his rightful inheritance emerged from his ordeal cynical, worldly, and mistrustful. He quickly came to detest presbyterianism and its clerical spokesmen; religious zeal, he felt, was itself often enough a mask, for the self-interest of the 'zealot'. Scottish aristocratic politicians were little better: bullies when they could be, toadies when they could not bully, and everlastingly greedy and ambitious. Scotland he loathed. He said when he got safely back to France that he would be hanged before he ever went to Scotland again, and he never did. He made one exception to his all-embracing dislike of Scotland and Scotsmen: for those who accompanied him on the forlorn adventure that led to the military débâcle at Worcester in September 1651. They all knew they were doomed. We 'are all laughing at the ridiculousness of our condition', wrote the duke of Hamilton, who was to die there, 'but we have one stout argument, despair; for we must now either stoutly fight it or die.' The king knew it too, and he never forgot those who went with him. Among them were Rothes and Lauderdale.

Charles owed his restoration to his three kingdoms to good luck. He had done nothing to help bring it about save to avoid committing any stupidity (like turning Catholic) and to outlive Oliver Cromwell. As a king he was immensely appealing to his subjects— a courteous, affable, accessible man of great charm, like his great-grandmother Mary Queen of Scots and his grandfather Henry IV. He had a genuine curiosity about many things, notably the practical uses of scientific discovery, and was prepared to discuss all sorts of topics—'shipping, architecture, bee-keeping, gardening, and urban pollution', writes Hutton, citing the diarist John Evelyn. He shared the tastes and pursuits of the people who counted in English society: tennis, hunting, horse-racing, the theatre, as well as some which became popular because he adopted them: fishing, yachting, and the bedding-down of members of that newest profession, female stage-players. His enthusiasm for the opposite sex was not limited to actresses, of course, and has left a misleading impression as to Charles's attentiveness to the business of being king. He was very conscious both of the need for exacting the deference due to his position and of those aspects of that position that set him off from other men, like touching for the king's evil. Though he hated routine, he was far from lazy; he regularly attended meetings of the privy council and of its policy-making body, the foreign affairs committee, and he was a good judge of political talent. He hated paperwork and vastly preferred to handle business orally. The efficiency of men like Arlington and Lauderdale in the handling of the paper-flow made them almost indispensable to Charles and caused him to overlook their occasional advocacy of policies he found unappealing.

Did he have any aims as king, any long-range objective that he kept constantly before his eye? Here the mask is hardest of all to penetrate. Charles was a cautious man, determined to do nothing to provoke a rebellion that might cause him to go on his travels again, as he put it. Some historians have argued that this was his sole objective, that all he wanted was to be comfortable. To say this is to take too little account of his deep sense of what kingship meant. Like his father and his father's father, he believed that to be a king was to rule. Like James VI and I—and unlike Charles I—he was prepared to draw back if necessary, to make concessions, to be patient. He knew that recent events had limited his options—in England he could not govern without parliament, as his father had attempted to do. But he meant to render parliament subservient if he could.

The depth of his belief in this sort of kingship is shown in the list of those he hated: from the leadership of the kirk to the earl of Shaftesbury, they were those who challenged his view of himself as king. The other side of this coin is his devotion to those who shared his blood: his brother, his sister, so miserably married in France, his much-put-upon wife whom in the end he would not put aside in order to have a legitimate heir, and his son young James, the prospective bridegroom.

The projected marriage could not take place until April 1663 at the earliest. Only then would both young people be of legal age, Anna twelve and James fourteen—there must be no repetition of the fiasco of 1659. In the meantime there was much to be done. For one thing, a message must be sent to Tweeddale, and it was. In the parliamentary session that had ended in July 1661 Tweeddale alone had had the courage, or unwisdom, to speak against the death penalty for a radical Covenanting minister named James Guthrie, on the ground that it was unfair to single out and punish one man for an offence so many had committed. Tweeddale's remarks had caused no adverse reaction at the time—they had been made before Lady Wemyss's offer to Charles—and after parliament adjourned Tweeddale was chosen to preside over the newly constituted privy council when the major officers of state and Rothes, its regular president, were absent. Now, however, the king seized upon them. On September 7 he ordered Tweeddale's arrest on account of his speeches. The earl was to be confined to Edinburgh Castle until further notice.

Tweeddale was dumbfounded—'thunderstruck' was the word he used in his letter to Lauderdale. He did not dispute the legality of Guthrie's death sentence, he said, but he felt that the 'disorders of the times' warranted some other punishment for him. He wrote a humble letter to the king—'Your majesty's displeasure was to me the messenger of death'—and asked his colleagues on the council for help. They rallied round him, writing to the king that he had carried himself as a 'faithful councillor and loyal subject'; Rothes was among the signatories of the letter. After two weeks the king freed him from the castle on the ground that the pregnant Lady Jean was near her time; he was to remain under house arrest at Yester until further notice. He was not released until May 1662, when parliament reconvened. Tweeddale had every right to be thunderstruck. The royal reaction far exceeded his alleged offence, especially given Charles's lack of touchiness where the speeches of English parliamentarians were concerned. He was being warned: do not cross the king, in parliament or anywhere else.*

Charles now began to manifest an interest in the reduction of Mary's marriage contract. In January 1662 he ordered Lauderdale to find out about it. Lauderdale wrote to Sir John Gilmour, the president of the court of session, seeking information: 'I neither know what was in the contract nor who proposes the reduction'—an indication that up to this point Lauderdale had not been involved in the affairs of the Buccleuch estate. Gilmour replied that the case had not been heard yet—it never would be—and that he had not seen the contract. He gathered from what he had heard that the arguments would stress two points. First, approval had not been given by a proper quorum of five tutors, since Haychesters, the fifth signatory tutor, had also signed on behalf of his minor son, and could not represent both parties. In the second place, when minors were parties to a grossly inequitable contract such as this, they and/or their heirs could ask the court to undo what had been done. In November 1662, after Haychesters and Tarras let the case against them go by default, the five tutors now opposed to the contract drew up a paper suggesting that there might have been malversation during the years of Mary's marriage, and that the estates of the tutors most deeply involved might be at risk. This, they wrote, might prove very advantageous to 'that noble person with whom this lady shall ally'. The tutors believed that Earl Francis' entail would be respected; under it 'that noble person' could acquire no part of the estate. They would soon be undeceived.

On February 1, 1662, Gilmour wrote to Tweeddale, still languishing under house arrest, telling him of Lauderdale's inquiry. He had talked to Rothes, who had made friendly noises about Tweeddale and remarked that the application for reduction would have some harsh things to say about both of them. Tweeddale replied, asking Gilmour to intercede with Rothes on his behalf and to see that justice was done in the 'intended match'. He himself would do everything

* In reflecting on this episode in his autobiography Tweeddale seemed especially miffed that Scottish officialdom—Rothes and the others—had accepted his hospitality at a 'splendid entertainment' at Pinkie House (one of his recent acquisitions from the Dunfermline estate) at the end of the parliamentary session, promoted his election as president of the council, and then went to London and denigrated him to the king. He commented 'that they had first made him a precedent and then an example'—a feeble enough attempt at wit.

The First Heiress: Mary Scott, countess of Buccleuch, 1647-1661. Married too young (aged 11), died too young (aged 13) of 'the cruells in her arm'. Her short, sad life did not spoil her sweet nature. (In a private Scottish collection.)

The Second Heiress: Anna Scott, countess, then duchess of Buccleuch, 1651-1723. Married at 12 to King Charles II's bastard son the Duke of Monmouth, she led a gilded, wretched life. (In a private Scottish collection.)

Their Father: Francis Scott, 2nd Earl of Buccleuch. A sickly young man who died at the age of 24 in 1651, leaving behind him the enormous, entailed estate which caused so much trouble. (In a private Scottish collection.)

Their Mother: Margaret Leslie, countess of Buccleuch, later countess of Wemyss. She buried three husbands and nine children, always knew what she wanted for herself and her family, and usually got it. (In a private Scottish collection.)

David, 2 Earl of Wemyss.

Their Stepfather: David, 2nd earl of Wemyss, who took Margaret Leslie as his third wife and never regretted it. A kind and loving father to Mary and Anna. (In a private Scottish collection.)

Their 'Wicked' Uncle: John Hay, 2nd earl of Tweeddale, husband to Francis Scott's sister Jean. He owed the Buccleuch family a lot of money and did not want to repay it. (By Sir Peter Lely, reproduced by courtesy of the Scottish National Portrait Gallery.)

The Politicians: John Leslie, 7th earl (later duke) of Rothes, Lord Chancellor of Scotland, Margaret Leslie's brother (by L. Schuneman, reproduced by courtesy of the Scottish National Portrait Gallery); and John Maitland, 2nd earl (later duke) of Lauderdale, Secretary of State for Scotland, with his second wife, Elizabeth Murray (by Sir Peter Lely, reproduced by permission of the Victoria & Albert Museum). Both hoped to find a way to dip into the Buccleuch fortune.

Prince Perkin: Charles II's eldest bastard, James, duke of Monmouth and Buccleuch. A beautiful, spoiled boy, married at 14 to Countess Anna, he always maintained that he was legitimate (The Royal Collection © Her Majesty the Queen). When his father died, he claimed the throne, and raised a rebellion - with the grisly result illustrated in King James VII and II's commemorative medal (below).

'just', if only Lady Wemyss could be persuaded to 'lay aside this implacable disposition'. Rothes had no intention of exerting himself for Tweeddale, but even if he had been disposed to do so, his sister would have paid no attention. She was not taking Rothes into her confidence—Rothes even believed, or so he said to Gilmour, that if the marriage went forward she would try to do something for Tarras, which was the last thing she intended to do. On February 15 Rothes wrote in exasperation to Lauderdale with the news that Lady Wemyss was planning to take Anna to London. Rothes thought this was a terrible idea. Anna was not a very strong child. Furthermore, she was recovering from smallpox, and the tell-tale marks had not yet vanished from her face. He implored Lauderdale to get the king to stop Lady Wemyss. He had gone to Wemyss Castle to find out what was planned, he wrote, but no one said a word to him.

Lady Wemyss had no intention of changing her plans. Nor had Charles any intention of stopping her: he wanted to see his prospective daughter-in-law. There was much for Lady Wemyss to do in London, and she intended to stay for some time once she and Anna got there. But she did wait until June to leave for the south. By that time the reduction of Mary's marriage contract had been accomplished. For another thing, if Anna was ill during the winter, it was wise to let the king see her at her best—Rothes' letter is our only indication that she had smallpox, which, if she had it, left her unmarked. One of the purposes of the trip was to put paid to rumours that Anna was afflicted with 'low stature, weakness and infirmities of body, and uncomeliness'—a pejorative way of indicating that Anna was below average height (like her half-sister Catherine), had recently been ill, and was far from dazzling—though in fact she was by no means uncomely. A month or so after Lady Wemyss and Anna arrived in London and settled into their lodgings in fashionable Henrietta Street, near Covent Garden, they had the chance to meet Anna's intended. Henrietta Maria, the queen mother, brought young James over from France to England. Samuel Pepys, who first saw him in September 1662, described him as 'a most pretty spark', who pleased both Henrietta Maria and Charles's newly-wedded wife, Catherine of Braganza.

The boy, wrote Pepys, 'doth hang much upon my Lady Castlemaine and is always with her'. James might be forgiven for this—his father's mistress was a stunning beauty—but his enthusiasm was a prefiguring of his future career as a womaniser. James and

Anna were brought together at court, where they could indulge their passion for dancing—Pepys thought that at the New Year's Eve ball Anna, whom he described as James's 'little mistress, which is very little', was one of the three best female dancers, Castlemaine being another. What opinion the two children formed of each other is not recorded.

Lady Wemyss's reasons for going to London were not merely personal and social, however. There was a pressing issue to be thrashed out: the legal implications of the fact that young James was a bastard. His illegitimacy would not prevent him from enjoying the income from the Buccleuch estate, but could his children inherit that estate? Could he make a valid will under Scots law? Lady Wemyss's lawyer, Sir Thomas Wallace, felt that for safety's sake he should be legitimised. But this raised another, enormously delicate issue: the attitude of the duke of York, the heir apparent. Lady Wemyss dared not offend the king's brother, but the question of young James's status had to be put. If his illegitimacy kept his and Anna's children from the inheritance, Tweeddale might yet win the game.

Charles was sufficiently concerned to summon Gilmour to London in September to discuss the question. They decided that the first step was to investigate precedents. The earl of Moray, the descendant of the most famous of Scotland's royal bastards, Mary Queen of Scots' half-brother the regent, ransacked his charter chest and found nothing. In December Gilmour, having returned home and conducted his own researches, reported that he could find no evidence that any king of Scotland ever legitimised any of his natural sons. Furthermore, legitimation was not necessary for young James to receive a peerage or an appointment to public office; there were no such precedents from the reign of James V, who had five bastard sons. A bastard could make a will. His children, provided they were legitimate, could inherit his estates. Even illegitimate children could be provided for by will. About the only thing a bastard could not do was dispose of movable property by will, but this problem was easily solved by making the necessary dispositions while all the parties were still alive. Only if a bastard died both intestate and without lawful issue would his property revert to the crown.

King Charles was 'very well pleased with what you write', Lauderdale informed Gilmour on January 23, 'and is resolved to do nothing in this business'. A draft drawn up at the end of 1662 giving 'James, Duke of Monmouth' the rights of a legitimate person with respect to the holding of honours, lands, and offices, and the disposal of his estate, but extending no further, was left unsigned. But Lady Wemyss was far from very well pleased. Under prodding from Wallace and from Haychesters, who in the hope of currying favour kept writing her unsolicited letters of advice, she kept pressing the king. 'Upon the solicitation of the Countess of Weems (*sic*),' wrote Lauderdale, the king summoned him 'and proposed that I would draw a paper giving [James] power to make a will and enjoy the dignity of a peer', without using the fateful word 'legitimation'. This was an idea that, at Wallace's behest, she had previously urged Gilmour to endorse. Lauderdale cried off: he was no lawyer. So, four days after he had declared that he would do nothing more, Charles gave way to Lady Wemyss's importunities. On January 27 Lauderdale conveyed the royal order to Gilmour, which Charles 'for some reason thought to be signified by me as his pleasure than to be under his own hand', so that his climbdown would seem less obvious. Gilmour was to convene an informal committee of seven: three judges, including himself, the lord advocate, and three leading lawyers, including Nisbet and Wallace, to discuss the points at issue. They agreed with Gilmour's previous judgment: nothing in writing was necessary at all. Lauderdale wrote Gilmour that Charles 'is very well pleased with the opinion you sent him, and rests satisfied with it'. He went on, pointedly: 'I have no further in command from his Majesty'. The matter was settled.*

Another matter that had to be settled before the marriage took place was Rothes' wardship. In October 1662 Wallace drafted a memorandum as to the possibilities, only one of which involved any real profit for the earl: a contract between himself and Anna, in which he would transfer the wardship to her in return for a consideration. Eventually this was done, but not quickly enough to keep Rothes from having a rather bad attack of nerves. The king, whose decision it was, moved slowly in the matter. Anna had long since been officially served heir to her estates, wardship or no wardship. Rothes came to London in January 1663, did not like what he found, and wrote a rather panicky letter to Gilmour three weeks before Anna's twelfth birthday. Suppose

---

* All this was conveyed in an official communication from Lauderdale. In a private letter to Gilmour on the same day Lauderdale referred to an 'old legitimation' that Lord Spynie had told Gilmour about. Lauderdale adjured Gilmour to 'get these parchments into your hand', send them, or a copy, to him, and keep the matter quiet. The implication was that the information must be kept from Lady Wemyss at all costs.

Anna turned twelve and the marriage took place before his contract was settled, he asked, what could be done to protect his interest? When the king finally acted, Rothes' relief was palpable. The king's 'kindness', he wrote Gilmour, was 'a greater advantage to me than all the sum I am to receive'. His enemies, who had sought 'to make my interest very insignificant', were foiled. 'I will make your ears tingle to hear how I have been dealt with.' Alas! we shall never know who those enemies were or what they did.

Rothes put a very high value on the king's kindness, because the sums he was to receive were enormous. His debts to the Buccleuch estate were cancelled—a total of 36,000 merks. In addition he was to receive £1,000 sterling a year for nine years—about ten per cent of the annual income of the estate. To secure this he was to be formally enfeoffed in land from the estate bringing in that much income. This was a huge payoff. The wardship of Anna's father, who also had come into the title as a minor, had been bought up in 1642 for 25,000 merks, about one eighth of what Anna was now obliged to pay. The contract was sent to Lady Wemyss. 'What her scruples may be I know not', wrote Rothes, 'but if she have any that may occasion the alteration of one sentence in that draft, I shall never sign.' Lady Wemyss and the others with responsibility for Anna's affairs, including the careful and scrupulous Bavielaw, signed on the dotted line. As Gilmour observed, they had no choice: Rothes' contract was drawn up on the king's orders. Rothes had done very well indeed.*

With respect to the other, more important, contract, that for the marriage itself, the king's requirements were clear. If, after the marriage, Anna predeceased her husband and left no children, James was to have the estate. This was an out-and-out violation of Earl Francis's entail, but Charles's attitude was understandable. Anna was apparently healthy enough, and had come through the bout of smallpox very well. But there were those rumours about her health, and

---

* After the marriage Anna's and Monmouth's curators challenged the legality of the wardship. Everything hinged on the status of one small piece of property which had originally been subject to wardship but whose status as such had been omitted in a regrant of the estate to Anna's great-grandfather in 1604. The issue was whether this was clerical oversight or whether King James VI deliberately intended to change the terms on which the property was held. The lawyers haggled at great length. In the final agreement, signed in 1669, Rothes got £8,000 sterling, two-thirds of the original amount. As she did with Mary's will, Anna sued her uncle's heirs in the 1690s on the ground that the grant of the wardship was wrongful.

the Scott family's record with respect to longevity was dismal. Anna's father had died young, as had three of his four brothers and sisters and three of his four children. Who was to say that Anna would not do so too? Wallace tried to satisfy the king; in October 1662 he presented a carefully drafted proposal that in some respects violated Scottish law and custom but did not immediately fracture the entail. The rule that a marriage had to last for a year and a day before a surviving spouse could lay claim to a lifetime income from a deceased spouse's estate might be waived in James's favour, 'providing that the granting thereof infer not her and her heirs their losing of the estate'. When Anna reached twenty-one she could dispose of the estate to James's heirs, failing offspring of her own, under the same conditions.

This did not satisfy Charles at all. The language was cloudy, indeed contradictory: how could James's heirs inherit without rupturing the entail? Furthermore, if Anna died childless before she reached her majority, James could not inherit the estate at all. So, in November, a new, considerably modified proposal appeared. If Anna died childless, James and his subsequent children would inherit. If he, too, died childless, then his heirs, not Anna's, would have the estate. Though the estate was now Anna's, she was obliged to give it up to the heir if she and James had children and he predeceased her, though she was guaranteed an income of £60,000 a year. All this was eventually written into the marriage contract, along with provisions which safeguarded Lady Wemyss's income from her jointure and the money Rothes would make from his contract. Thus was Earl Francis's entail destroyed, though in other respects it was adhered to: young James took the name and arms of Scott of Buccleuch. The king, for his part, promised to spend £40,000 sterling on the purchase of Scottish land for James and his descendants, so that he would not, like Tarras, come empty-handed to the marriage. This land would revert to the crown if James died childless, though Anna might keep the income for her lifetime if she survived him—an academic provision, as it turned out, since Charles never bought any land. He did give his son a less expensive wedding present in November 1662, making him a duke, duke of Monmouth in the English peerage,* with precedence

---

* Among young James's string of titles was that of Baron Fotheringhay. This was an extraordinary decision, since Fotheringhay was a place of ill omen. Richard III had been born there, and James's great-great-grandmother, Mary Queen of Scots, had lost her head there. There were second thoughts: James became Baron Tynedale on the issue of the formal patent in January 1663.

over all other dukes except the king's brother. In doing this Charles ignored both the opinion of his mother and the advice of his lord chancellor, the earl of Clarendon, who thought the title of earl of Buccleuch enough for James. Clarendon commented sourly in his memoirs that Lady Castlemaine, now at the height of her influence, was very enthusiastic about the award of a dukedom. No doubt: she had royal bastards of her own to think of. Anna's prospective husband might be a duke, but she was still only a countess, and was so described in the marriage contract.

The proposed terms of the contract produced much comment. Haychesters was still hopeful of finding some advantage for himself and his disinherited son in the projected marriage—perhaps Tarras could sell his supposed claims to Monmouth for cash. So he wrote an ingratiating letter to Lady Wemyss, warning her that since the proposed contract violated the entail, it could activate the 'clause irritant', the clause that extruded a female holder of the estate who attempted to alter the entail. If Anna signed this contract, she could be deprived and Lady Tweeddale put in possession. Haychesters urged Lady Wemyss to be very careful, and get legal advice from people not beholden to Tweeddale, who would try to trap her by making light of her fears until it was too late.

Lady Wemyss consulted the lawyers. They were very forthright: the contract violated the entail, and the 'clause irritant' would come into play when Anna, having signed the contract as a minor, reached her majority unless, in the meanwhile, she acted to restore the entail. If she died childless before reaching her majority, the heir under the entail would have two principal options: either suing to reduce Monmouth's rights, or pursuing Anna's curators* and all the others who had signed the contract for damages equalling the total value of the estate. The latter course was the more likely, the lawyers thought, since the heir would probably prefer not to challenge the king's son. The only other suggestion the lawyers had was that Charles might use his power of revocation to nullify the entail on the ground that it violated the earlier custom of the Buccleuch estates, which required that they pass to male heirs. The obvious

---

* On February 11, 1663, her twelfth birthday, Anna formally nominated her curators, who were officially responsible for the management of her affairs until she reached twenty-one. There were thirteen in all, headed by Rothes and Wemyss. Three of her former tutors, Harden, Bavielaw, and Eliot, were included; Haychesters and the troublemaking Scotstarvit were not.

objection to this proposal was that the only living male descendants of the first earl of Buccleuch were Tweeddale's sons; understandably, no more was heard of it. Lady Wemyss had also inquired about Tarras; the lawyers opined that the wisest course was to pay him off in return for his renunciation of his rights, before he made any mischief.

Whatever the merits of the lawyers' arguments, they were ignored and the contract drawn up in accordance with the king's wishes. His son would have the estate if Anna died childless. As far as Lady Wemyss was concerned, she did not care what happened to the estate under those circumstances, as long as Tweeddale did not get it. But the curators were nervous, especially those who had been members of the former council of tutors, and were thus obliged by Earl Francis's will to maintain the entail. On April 15, 1663, five days before the wedding, Gilmour wrote a long letter to Lauderdale reporting that he had attended a meeting of Anna's curators and lawyers called by Lord Chancellor Glencairn. Bavielaw expressed grave reservations. He had sworn to uphold the entail: how could he now consent to its fracturing? How could Gilmour himself approve of this, since he had drafted the original entail at Earl Francis's direction? Gilmour's response was a masterpiece of equivocation: the president of Scotland's highest court was in a very awkward position indeed. He explained to Bavielaw that Charles had named him and Lauderdale to represent Monmouth in the drafting of the contract—Monmouth had no curators because as yet he had no estate. What was proposed was so advantageous for Monmouth that, Gilmour said, he could not oppose it: 'it was not our part to stand in the way of such propositions'. The contract made no specific mention of the entail. Monmouth's liferent in the estate, and the rights of the heirs of the marriage, were secure in any case; 'what further was pressed for the Countess of Buccleuch by her mother and lawyers . . . had been ill service to refuse. The thing is in the King's power and (blessed be God) he is a just and good King. I conceive . . . the thing was primarily intended by my Lady Wemyss in favor of the Duke of Monmouth . . . not without some odium to others', though even she was nervous about breaking the entail. Bavielaw was convinced, and signed the contract—but Gilmour himself did not. As Monmouth's agent he could not advise rejection of the contract, but as the drafter of the original entail, he would not 'be witness against my former witnessing'. This was extraordinary. In the end only two of Anna's thirteen curators withheld their signatures.*

On April 20, 1663, the Monday after Easter, a day of pouring rain—not the happiest of auguries—Anna and James were married in the King's Chamber at Whitehall. It was the social event of the season, attended by the king and queen and all the court. Earl David provided the wedding feast; the day ended with supper and dancing at Monmouth's lodgings in Hedge Lane, off Charing Cross. To mark the occasion Charles raised the earldom of Buccleuch to a duchy, the third dukedom in Scotland.[†] The observant Samuel Pepys noticed that the coat of arms at the tail of the young duke's coach contained no bar sinister, an oversight remedied two days later. Lady Wemyss and King Charles were very pleased. At no cost to himself the king had provided for his beloved James's financial future. Lady Wemyss and her daughter were now allied with royalty, and Anna had avoided the dreadful fate of falling into Tweeddale's clutches. What the bride and groom thought about it all we do not know, nor is it likely that anyone thought to ask them. Their destiny had been determined before they ever met.

Anna, like her sister, was married as a child. As in Mary's case, the adults who controlled the children's fate believed a prompt wedding to be desirable. If Anna died before she married, Lady Tweeddale would inherit the estate, something neither Lady Wemyss nor King Charles wished to see happen. By contrast with Mary's case, the legality of Anna's marriage was undeniable, and so it did not require immediate consummation. The bedding-down after the wedding was *pro forma*; as Charles wrote to his sister on the day, 'We intend to dance and see them abed together, but the ceremony shall stop there, for they are both too young to lie all night together'. Earl David's diary indicates that the mar-

---

* Lauderdale, like Gilmour, did not sign the contract, but for a different reason. He had a claim to a piece of property specifically mentioned in the contract as part of the Buccleuch estate; if he signed, he would prejudice his claim. The contract runs to twenty-one printed pages in Fraser's *Scotts of Buccleuch*; over fourteen are devoted to a detailed listing of the property of the estate.

† The grant of 1663 limited the dukedom to Monmouth's children. If he had none, the next holder after Anna would be only an earl. In 1666 Charles made Anna duchess in her own right, so that her heirs, if descended from a subsequent marriage, would be dukes.

riage was consummated on February 9, 1665, two days before Anna's fourteenth birthday. A month later Lauderdale observed that they 'lie nightly together'.

The behaviour of King Charles and Lady Wemyss in arranging this early marriage was self-interested, to be sure, but not thoughtless or cruel by the standards of the seventeenth century. Aristocrats married early, especially aristocratic girls, and princesses too, everywhere in Europe. Margaret Tudor was sent north at fourteen to marry King James IV. Mary Queen of Scots married at fifteen. So did King Charles's grandmother, Anne of Denmark, his mother, Henrietta Maria, his sister Henrietta, his sister-in-law Mary of Modena, and his niece who ultimately became Queen Mary II. His sister Mary, the mother of Mary II's husband William III, was married to William II of Orange at the age of ten and was installed as William's wife at thirteen. James VI, who waited until he was twenty-three to marry, publicly expressed his irritation at the stories that went around about this delay, which 'bred in the breasts of many a great jealousy of my inability, as if I were a barren stock'.

Such early marriages were equally common for the daughters of the Scottish aristocracy. Lady Wemyss's exact age at her first marriage in 1635 is not known, but she was probably in her mid-teens—her brother Rothes was five at the time—and she married her daughter by her first husband to Lord Melville when she was fifteen and he eighteen. Rothes' brother-in-law, under discussion as a husband for Anna in 1659, was fifteen in that year. Rothes was married at eighteen, Lauderdale at sixteen. Lauderdale's mother was fifteen at her wedding; his aunt Anne Maitland, whom he never knew, was married at thirteen to the second earl of Winton, who went mad on their wedding night. Anne died six years later, still a virgin. Tweeddale's experience, described in Chapter 2, was typical: he was eighteen, Lady Jean fifteen. That they were happy indicates that an early marriage could work well. Many, including that of Anna and Monmouth, did not.

What choice did prospective brides and grooms have? Did their feelings matter to anyone other than themselves? Were they consulted? Could either party refuse to go through with a proposed marriage and make the refusal stick? Lawrence Stone, in his book on *The Family, Sex, and Marriage in England*, 1500–1800, declares that the daughters of the landed classes 'married on the average at about twenty in the late sixteenth century, rising to about twenty-two to twenty-three in the late seventeenth and eighteenth'. This relatively high age of marriage in England was owing in part to 'a greater willingness by parents to allow their children rather more freedom of mate choice'. This of course entailed 'allowing them to reach maturity before being obliged to make up their minds'. He says elsewhere in the book, however, that 'authoritarian control by parents over the marriages of their children . . . lasted longest in the richest and most aristocratic circles', and that amongst the Scottish aristocracy this control, which he describes as 'high-handed but now archaic', continued 'unimpaired well into the mid-eighteenth century'.

Antonia Fraser, in *The Weaker Vessel*, her book on English women in the seventeenth century, declares that after the Restoration 'parents in general no longer believed in exercising absolute authority over their children in the making of a match'. She then cites the case of a young member of the gentry class, the sixteen-year-old Alice Sherard, who was carefully told that she did not have to marry her aunt's husband's nephew and heir, but that if she did not, she would not receive the thousand pieces of gold the uncle was prepared to leave her in his will. Alice went through with the marriage.

Fraser also describes with considerable relish the case of Elizabeth Percy, only child of the last earl of Northumberland, a great heiress whose father died when she was three. When she reached the legal age of consent her grandmother arranged her marriage to the thirteen-year-old heir of the duke of Newcastle. He died in a few months, whereupon the old lady in effect sold her granddaughter to the disreputable Thomas Thynne of Longleat, known as 'Tom of the Ten Thousand', a wealthy landowner and friend of the duke of Monmouth. Young Elizabeth, now fourteen, wanted no part of him. She signed the marriage contract, and then ran away before the marriage could be consummated. She had a Swedish wooer, Count Königsmark, who arranged for three of his servants to ambush Thynne and kill him. The leader of the group claimed that he was seeking only to provoke a duel, a story rendered somewhat doubtful by the fact that one of his colleagues fired a blunderbuss at Thynne through the window of his coach, leaving five bullets in him. Königsmark escaped the gallows—though his servants did not—and renewed his suit. Alas for all his useful work: in 1682, at the age of fifteen, Elizabeth Percy married her third (and last) husband, the nineteen-year-old duke of Somerset. She was a great heiress, like Mary and Anna, and like them she was married as a child. There the resemblance ends. Somerset was a good husband to her; they had a happy marriage of forty years and thirteen children.

The examples Stone cites from the seventeenth century have little enough to do with free choice on the part of the young women involved. There was the orphaned daughter of the mayor of Abingdon, for instance, sold when she was thirteen to be the bride of Sir Edmund Verney's sixteen-year-old son and heir. There was Alice Wandesford, coerced at twenty-four in 1651 into a marriage with a man she had never seen, a match arranged by her uncle in order to salvage part of the family estate. She went through with it, and on the afternoon of her wedding day became violently ill, an illness Stone regards as psychosomatic. There was the daughter of the earl of Newburgh, whom Stone defines as a member of 'the high aristocracy in the north' rather than as a Scot, which he was. The girl was two years older than Anna. She was brought to Charles's court at fourteen, rejected one projected husband because he was Catholic, but was not permitted to marry the young man she fell in love with because both families disapproved. Eventually she agreed to marry a man her father selected for her, provided that £1,000 sterling she had inherited went to the payment of her debts at court rather than to her husband as part of her dowry. The marriage was miserable: he drank and she scolded. There was Lady Jemima Montagu, daughter of the earl of Sandwich, who at nineteen was pushed into marriage with the son of Sir George Carteret, her father's colleague in the navy. Pepys, who acted as go-between in introducing the young people to each other, noted that Lady Jemima, a great favourite of his, was 'mighty sad' on her wedding day. (It might be mentioned that Pepys himself married a fifteen-year-old and by his own admission treated her shabbily.) One marriage Stone does not mention is that of Carteret's grandson, married in 1675 at the age of eight to a little girl the same age.

On the other hand it should be pointed out that the most notorious case of marital failure in the Restoration period, that of Lord and Lady Roos, was not a result of child marriage, nor, apparently, of coercion. The difficulty was that she enjoyed sex, while he did—or could—not. And he drank. The inevitable happened: Lady Roos gave birth to a son, named Ignotus after his father. The upshot was a scandalous and unprecedented divorce case, heard in the House of Lords. King Charles was regularly present; it was, he said, as much fun as going to the theatre.

As for Scotland, Rosalind Marshall in *Virgins and Viragos*, her history of Scottish women, echoes Fraser rather than Stone. In reference to the later seventeenth century she writes, 'The day when parents could hope to arrange their children's marriages quietly, with no reference to the young people themselves, had long since passed'. This comment applies accurately to the family Marshall knows best, that of Anne, duchess of Hamilton, but not to others. Marshall herself admits that 'Girls from reasonably wealthy families . . . believed that they must submit to their families' wishes'. There are cases of aristocratic girls marrying men of their own choice in spite of opposition from the family—Marshall cites that of the earl of Moray's sister, who in 1640 married the laird of Freuchie while her brother was away in London. She then successfully mollified Moray, who agreed to hand over her dowry. But Tweeddale's marriage is far more typical: that of two teenagers who had seen each other but never spoken together when their marriage was arranged.

Marshall also declares that 'By the mid-seventeenth century child marriages had become a thing of the past, abandoned by even the most mercenary in the face of public disapproval'. The accuracy of this statement depends on one's definition of a child. Were Mary and Anna children? One might think so. Certainly they took no part in the decisions as to their destiny, though it suited Lady Wemyss to declare that Mary was eager to wed young Haychesters in order to excuse the illegality of the marriage. A much sadder cautionary tale even than Mary's is provided by Lady Wemyss's granddaughter, Margaret Leslie, countess of Leven.

Alexander Leslie, Lady Wemyss's only son by her first marriage, succeeded his famous grandfather, General Alexander Leslie, as earl of Leven in 1661. He was a worthless young man who died in 1664 at the age of twenty-seven. According to John Lamont the diarist he died of a fever brought on by a colossal drinking bout with the earl of Dundee, a much older man. The two were said to have toasted each other in sea water as they crossed the Forth between Queensferry and Inverkeithing, following this up with bumpers of sack when they reached land. Leven left three small daughters behind him. Like Earl Francis he had entailed his estate the year before his death. If his daughters all died without issue, his lands and his earldom were to pass to the second son of his uncle Rothes. If Rothes had no second son, the next in line was the second son of Leven's sister Catherine and her husband Lord Melville. Margaret, the eldest daughter, became countess of Leven at the age of four. Rothes, her great-uncle and the principal member of her council of tutors, insisted, when she reached the age of marriage, that she marry his nephew, a brother of the earl of Eglinton, the same man who had been under discussion in 1660 as a possible husband for Anna. Margaret did not want to do this, and explained herself in a letter to her aunt Catherine, her father's sister, on July 31, 1673:

> Be assured I shall give my consent to be married to no man till I be twenty years of age, and then I hope in God I shall not be in great danger of bearing bairns. I got word from Dr. Waderburn that if I married now I should hazard both my own life and my child's . . . I believe it's only the chancellor's [Rothes'] desire to get him this fortune and me to die, and there-fore . . . [this is] a matter I ought to consider upon ere I weaken the family my great-grandfather got at the price of his blood.

This was a prophetic letter, but Margaret's resistance did her no good. Within three months the marriage contracts were signed. Margaret survived for a little over a year; she died at fifteen in November 1674. One of her two sisters predeceased her; the other, who succeeded as countess of Leven, died unmarried at thirteen in 1676. Rothes immediately tried to lay hands on the earldom in the name of the heir, his second son, who did not exist. Lord Melville, who did have a second son, resisted this: he and everyone else knew that Rothes would simply loot the estate. Lauderdale, on whose backing everything depended, supported Melville, who became curator in the name of his second son David. No final settlement was possible until Rothes died, which he did in 1681, leaving no sons of any kind. The earldom then passed to David, who eventually inherited the Melville estates as well.

A less tragic tale, but one equally illustrative of the Leslie family's cold-blooded eye to the main chance, is that of Lady Wemyss's last child, also a Margaret, born in 1659. She was one of two of Lady Wemyss's five children by Earl David who survived infancy. The other was a son, David, Lord Elcho, who, sadly, died in 1671 at the age of sixteen. Lady Wemyss then induced Earl David to settle his title and estates on Margaret, cutting out his elder daughter (by his first wife), who was married to the earl of Sutherland. The argument she used was that only thus could the name of Wemyss be preserved—there was conveniently at hand a kinsman, James Wemyss, for Margaret to marry. And married she was, on Christmas day 1671, one week before her thirteenth birthday. In due course she became countess of Wemyss in her own right, and successfully fended off her half-sister's many efforts to overturn Earl David's dispositions. Her marriage seems to have worked out well enough, but it is notable that when her own children came along she did not emulate her mother. Lord Montgomery, Eglinton's son, was a suitor for her daughter Margaret; she praised the young man to Margaret to no avail. And after some initial resistance she gave in to Margaret and agreed to her marriage to the earl of Northesk. But, as she herself said, no suitor could prevail 'except he gain my consent'. All three of her children were married in their teens. The elder daughter, Anna, was married at fifteen in 1691 to David, earl of Leven, aged thirty-one, the ultimate beneficiary of Rothes' manipulation of the Leven inheritance, and, like his wife, a grandchild of Lady Wemyss.

Stone's observation that parents were allowing their children more latitude in the selection of marriage partners can be accepted as largely correct for the eighteenth century, even in Scotland, though there were still brides of Lammermoor there. The examples Stone cites in his chapter on 'The Companionate Marriage' are drawn almost exclusively from that period. Parent and child in effect each had a veto. Squire Western would not compel his daughter Sophia to marry the odious Blifil, but he would not permit her to marry her true love, the bastard Tom Jones, until Tom turned out to be a high-born bastard with a fortune. But in the age of Charles II the older pattern prevailed. Daughters, and sons too, married whom they were told to marry, and the girls married young. Mary and Anna Scott were younger than most, to be sure, for the reasons given in this tale. But save for the illegality of Mary's marriage one can hardly call them exceptions to the normal practices of the upper classes on both sides of the Tweed.

6

An Illegal Act of Parliament

A few weeks after Anna's wedding her stepfather Earl David returned to Scotland to attend parliament. Lady Wemyss was in no hurry to go back, however—not until she could take Anna with her. Anna and James were too young to live as husband and wife. Until that time came—and Lady Wemyss saw no reason to hasten it—Anna should live at home, in Wemyss Castle, preferably until she was twenty-one. Her husband, in the meantime, might well be sent abroad, at his father's expense, to complete his education. The beauty of this plan was that Lord and Lady Wemyss would continue to collect the income of the Buccleuch estates on Anna's behalf. Charles rejected Lady Wemyss's idea out of hand. He had no intention of allowing either his beloved son or Anna to leave court—he and his solemn brother had both taken a great liking to their new kinswoman. And as for the money: that was for the young people to enjoy. Monmouth was extravagant and had already accumulated considerable debt. The days of prosperity at Wemyss Castle fuelled by Buccleuch money were over. As a form of consolation Charles gave Lady Wemyss a pension of £500 sterling a year, the same amount as the tutors had officially allotted her to raise the children. In recent years she had been collecting at least three times that much from the estate.

Lady Wemyss was disappointed. She also, once more, began to get nervous about her bugbear Tweeddale. She had not forgotten what the lawyers had said about the marriage contract, the violated entail, and its clause irritant. And to her dismay the kaleidoscope of Scottish politics had led to an enormous improvement in Tweeddale's position in recent months. The rising star now was Secretary of State Lauderdale, who was Tweeddale's first cousin. The stupidity of the men Charles had entrusted with carrying out his agenda in Edinburgh had thrown Lauderdale and Tweeddale together, and they were now political allies.

John Maitland, second earl and only duke of Lauderdale, has a claim, along with that great Covenanter the marquis of Argyll, to be the most important Scottish politician of the seventeenth century. Politics was in his blood. His grandfathers, John Maitland of Thirlestane and Alexander Seton, earl of Dunfermline, were the two most important lord chancellors of the reign of James VI. As early as 1640, when he was only twenty-four, he accompanied the Scots commissioners appointed to negotiate with Charles I to London, thanks to his uncle, the second earl of Dunfermline, who was one of them. His skills as a negotiator made him an invaluable and increasingly influential member of the ruling junto's inner circle. He supported the Scottish intervention on the side of the English rebels against Charles I, but after the king's defeat his attitude began to change. He wanted to be both a good presbyterian and a good royalist, but if he were forced to choose, he, like most of his class, would opt for the king.

So Lauderdale became a principal contriver of the Engagement of 1647. He was the envoy sent to Prince Charles in the summer of 1648 to persuade the young man to come to Scotland to join the Engager army. Thus he and his future master met for the first time. Lauderdale was impressed. 'We are like to be very happy in him,' he wrote to his political ally the future duke of Hamilton, now secretary of state. From the beginning the experienced politician of thirty-two and the youth of eighteen got on well together. Lauderdale quickly learned that personal contact with Charles was the key to having influence with him. For the next three years Lauderdale was in and out of Charles's company a good deal. He had an impressive presence—a large, red-haired, red-faced man, a persuasive talker, a wit and a raconteur who, said one of his English critics, often spoiled his jokes in the telling. Like both his grandfathers he was a learned man who carried his learning lightly. Charles enjoyed his company and listened to his advice, to the irritation of the future earl of Clarendon, whose distrust and dislike of him began at this time. Lauderdale accompanied Charles to Scotland in 1650, and in 1651 to Worcester, where he was captured. He spent the next nine years in an English prison.

The years in prison whetted Lauderdale's appetite for wealth and power. Public office was the key to both, as was true everywhere in seventeenth-century Europe. Lauderdale knew it, and his single-minded pursuit of these twin objectives never wavered after 1660.

His extensive correspondence with his man of business in Edinburgh, William Sharp, the brother of the archbishop of St. Andrews, amply illustrates his financial concerns and his frequent cash-flow problems. As for power, the only path was royal favour, to get it and keep it. Lauderdale's aim was monopoly. All Scottish patronage would flow through him. He would have no political rivals in either Edinburgh or London: on Scottish matters the king would consult only with him and with those whose loyalty to him was beyond question. By the middle of 1667 he achieved his goal, and maintained his grip for over a decade. He was the most successful politician, and longest-serving officeholder, of the reign of Charles II in any of his three kingdoms.

By Anna's wedding day Lauderdale had made some progress toward the power he craved. The royal commissioner in Edinburgh, the earl of Middleton, who was Clarendon's man, bungled an attempt to drive Lauderdale, and all those he thought might possibly be helpful to Lauderdale, from public life. Tweeddale was on Middleton's enemies' list, as was the earl of Crawford, Rothes' father-in-law. Charles was greatly irritated. Lauderdale's speech driving the final nails into Middleton's political coffin took place at a meeting of the king's Scottish council at Whitehall on April 20, 1663, the day of Anna's wedding. Clarendon, who told Middleton that he had acted like a madman, observed that now Lauderdale was firmly established in office. He was right.

Hitherto Lauderdale, though not unfriendly, had kept Tweeddale at arm's length politically. Cousin though he was, Tweeddale's Cromwellian past did not make him a political asset. Lauderdale had done nothing to help Tweeddale when the king ordered his arrest in September 1661, remaining impervious to Lady Tweeddale's letters to him on her husband's behalf. He also ignored the letter Lady Jean wrote him in February 1662 against the injustice to herself she anticipated in the marriage contract. 'I have long borne the reproach of my father's family by the practices of the mother and servants of it,' she wrote, and now there were these 'diligent endeavors used to stop the prosecution of justice and the laws'. She was prepared to bow to the king's wishes, she said, but she wanted Lauderdale to preserve her husband and herself from injury and calumny. It was a rather muddled letter. Whatever Lauderdale may have thought of it, he was not going to oppose the king's plans for Monmouth's financial security for Lady Tweeddale's sake. Nor, prior to Middleton's attempt to ruin them both, was he prepared to associate with Tweeddale. But now Tweeddale became a useful political ally for Lauderdale. So too, was Rothes, who had been carefully non-committal throughout the attack on Lauderdale, but who did not care for Middleton's attempt to purge Crawford, who was his foster-father as well as his father-in-law.

By the summer of 1663 Tweeddale was again president of the privy council. His growing political stature, and his association with Lauderdale, made Lady Wemyss very nervous. Fertile in expedients as always, she thought of a remedy, one that had first emerged in the form of a question in one of the many papers the lawyers had generated before the final drafting of the marriage contract: could the entail be broken by act of parliament? Parliament was now in session; it reconvened on June 18, 1663. Earl David had gone home to attend it, and Lauderdale to Edinburgh to manage it—his first visit to Scotland since leaving it in Charles's company on the road to Worcester in 1651. If parliament confirmed the marriage contract, and also blocked any future legal challenge to it, the entail would remain broken, and Tweeddale's hopes obliterated forever. So Lady Wemyss went to the king.

On July 2, 1663, Lauderdale's (and Charles's) friend Sir Robert Moray, who had rather reluctantly agreed to serve as acting Scottish secretary at court while Lauderdale was in Scotland—Sir Robert had no political ambitions—wrote to Lauderdale about that day's conversation with the king. 'The first thing his Majesty said to me was that there was a paper presented to him (which he put into my hand) wherein it was desired that [the] contract of the D. of Monmouth's marriage might be confirmed by an Act of Parlt. in the terms you see in the copy of the paper', which Moray enclosed. Charles 'said the thing is perhaps not necessary, yet abundance of law does not break it. You will soon see what is to be done in the case'.

Moray's news was most unwelcome to Lauderdale, who was feeling harassed. 'No dog leads so busy a life,' he wrote. 'Torment of visitors in crowds, not companies, and incessant meetings . . . I am perfectly dazed.' Managing the parliament was far from easy. There was a long agenda of religious, military, and economic legislation to be dealt with, and the political mess Middleton had made required cleaning up. What was worse was that the king had sent him north without any special powers. Rothes, not he, had succeeded Middleton as royal commissioner, which meant that Rothes had to be included in every

initiative. Middleton, meanwhile, was still in London, intriguing to recover his position. Lauderdale knew that Moray was dependable, since
he had also been on Middleton's enemies list, but whether the comparatively apolitical Sir Robert could handle all the intrigue at court was
not at all clear. Lauderdale, though he longed to be back in London—'God send me . . . to Whitehall again,' he wrote to Moray on
July 7, at the same time asking for his spectacles—professed not to
worry. He had heard 'great brags' in Edinburgh about Charles's renewed favour to Middleton, he wrote shortly after his arrival, but 'I
am sure he [Charles] will not let me be bit to death by a duck'.

Getting Monmouth's marriage contract ratified in parliament
might be very difficult. This was a parliament of landowners; this
contract carried a not-so-veiled threat to their control of their own
estates. It would set a very dangerous precedent: if parliament could
destroy Earl Francis's entail at the king's behest, it could destroy anyone's. Lauderdale's first move, when he received Moray's letter,
was to go, with Rothes, who had also been sent a copy of Lady
Wemyss's proposal, to consult Sir John Gilmour. Gilmour 'admired at the proposition', and said that he wanted to consult all the
members of the court of session. 'This,' wrote Lauderdale, 'we
found absolutely best.' The judges swiftly delivered a unanimous
opinion. 'Such an act could not pass in parliament to make void entails, as to be excepted out of the act *salvo juris cuiuslibet* which is the
security of subjects in cases of ratifications of private rights.'* It
would be most unfair for parliament to prohibit future legal chal-
lenges to a private act, since it would not have heard all sides of the
case; this was 'most unfit to be pressed by his Majesty'. The judges,
Lauderdale wrote, were very pleased at the sense of fairness the king
had shown by consulting them before he issued any orders. Their
written opinion would arrive in due course—it followed a week later—but Lauderdale wanted to let Moray know what it would be,
in order to 'prevent further importunities upon his Majesty'.

The judges' reaction to Lady Wemyss's proposal was hardly surprising. It advocated three unprecedented actions. Parliament had

---

* Almost every session of the Scottish parliament saw the passage of a number
of 'private' acts, ratifying grants and other favours to private individuals and
corporations such as towns and universities. Parliament also passed, as the final
act of each session, the act *salvo juris cuiuslibet*. This act declared that none of the
private acts passed during the session prejudiced the legal rights of others, and
gave anyone who felt aggrieved the right to sue in court.

never before been asked to ratify a marriage contract between two of the king's subjects. Parliament had never nullified an entail. And parliament had never barred anyone whose legal rights were adversely affected by a private act from recourse to justice. Small wonder that Lauderdale wanted this proposal to die a quick death.

So did Moray. 'When the result of the conference with the lords of the session comes,' he wrote in reply, 'he [Charles] will stop their mouths with it that made those absurd proposals.' And so, apparently, it turned out. When Moray delivered the judges' written opinion, Charles accepted it, 'and so, I think, hath rid himself of the lady's importunity', which weighed on him 'as much as anything but her humor and way of dealing'. Clearly Charles did not like Lady Wemyss. This bossy and formidable intriguer was in every respect the opposite of the beautiful Lady Frances Stuart, currently Charles's idea of the *pièce de résistance* of womanhood and soon to be the quarry of a courtiers' committee to 'get' her for the king.* Charles called Lady Wemyss a rumourmonger. He told Moray that she was the source of the stories going around Whitehall to the effect that Lauderdale was plotting against Clarendon and had said unkind things about Monck—'damned, insipid lies', Lauderdale called them when he heard them.

Moray had underestimated Lady Wemyss's persistence and tactical skill, however. It was difficult for anyone to get the giddy adolescent Monmouth to pay attention to anything serious, but in this case Lady Wemyss did so, since the ratification of the contract was so obviously in his interest. She prodded him into writing Earl David, asking him to remind Rothes and Lauderdale about the king's wish that the contract be ratified—and she knew that Charles loved his son very much. So, after a day or two, Charles brought up the subject with Moray once again. He had not thought clearly about the judges' reasoning before, he said, but now he found it puzzling, since the English parliament 'can cut off entails'. Moray tried; Charles seemed satisfied; two days later he wanted a further explanation of the act *salvo*. Moray did his best, arguing also against the usefulness of any parliamentary action, since what one parliament can do another can undo. Moray urged Lauderdale to write something like

---

* Frances never succumbed, and eventually eloped with Charles's cousin the duke of Lennox, to the king's intense annoyance. She has her form of immortality: she was the model for the figure of Britannia, which first appeared on English copper coins in this reign.

this to the king, who, Moray opined, would be 'glad to see it'. He also asked Lauderdale to get a lawyer or judge to provide a clarification of the act *salvo* for Charles; it needed 'a better lawyer than myself to make it perfectly clear to him'.

This letter of Moray's was written on July 23. On that day the king escorted his wife to Tunbridge Wells, where she was to take the waters, an annual ritual with Queen Catherine, who liked the place. Charles spent the next few weeks going back and forth between London and Tunbridge and paying a visit to the docks at Portsmouth, and for that brief time there was no more talk of the marriage contract. But in mid-August Charles brought the matter up again. He was not satisfied with Moray's explanations, and, he said, he had information that Lauderdale himself had had a confirmation passed by parliament excepting his lordship of Musselburgh from the act *salvo*. Moray replied that the judges' exposition was clear. 'After this his Majesty did not insist, but I expect he will be pressed to drive it on further.' Moray hunted through Lauderdale's papers and could find nothing relevant on Musselburgh; he urged Lauderdale to clear the matter up rapidly, 'against the time the Duke's case be insisted on'.

Before Lauderdale could reply to this, Charles acted. On August 20 he wrote a cross letter, not to Lauderdale or Rothes, but to Lord Chancellor Glencairn, who as one of Middleton's allies was not in good odour, scolding him and Gilmour severely for their behaviour over the contract. They had assured him that it was legally valid when it was signed, and now, when he wanted parliament to ratify it, they had told him that it was 'inconsistent with the law'. Furthermore, they had suggested no way out of this dilemma. If nothing was done before parliament rose, not only would Monmouth gain nothing from the marriage if he outlived Anna, but both of them, and the curators, would be in legal jeopardy. Charles, in writing this, was in effect conceding the illegality of the contract. He told Glencairn that he expected prompt action to remedy this situation. 'And . . . since I see that the exception of the act *salvo jure* is passed in some cases . . . therefore I do expect in this.' He also demanded an accounting of 'that great fortune from the time it ought to be accounted for'. The king's purpose, and his displeasure, were plain. Whatever reservations the lawyers might have, he wanted parliament to act, to safeguard Monmouth's fortune and future.

Glencairn and Gilmour were terrified. Gilmour at once wrote a defensive letter to Moray, which he wanted Moray to show to

Charles along with his letter of the previous April to Lauderdale explaining why he had not witnessed the marriage contract—he enclosed a copy. He had always acted in Monmouth's interest, he said; he certainly could not 'be thought to have gratified any pretended [!] heirs of tailzie, to whose prejudice (if law will allow it) the contract of marriage is concluded'. The judges as a group, however, Gilmour among them, stood their ground. After some days of deliberation they reiterated that the marriage contract could not secure the estate to Monmouth failing heirs to the marriage, though he could enjoy the income for life if the marriage lasted a year and a day. Parliamentary ratification of the contract would 'altogether invert the fundamental law of the kingdom'. Tweeddale's consent would make no difference. Unless the law itself were changed, Tweeddale's son 'or any other next heir of tailzie might justly challenge' the marriage contract. At the same time Sir John Nisbet, Tweeddale's lawyer, prepared an opinion on the act *salvo* for the king. The case of Lauderdale's lordship of Musselburgh was not relevant, Nisbet wrote, because Musselburgh was church property: it had been part of the lands of the abbey of Dunfermline, which had been permanently annexed to the crown. So the king was acting to his own prejudice in consenting to the exception of Musselburgh from the act *salvo*. He could do that, but he could not similarly prejudice the rights of his subjects.

Lauderdale and Rothes, who was still at odds with his sister, clearly hoped that these weighty legal opinions would cause Charles to change his mind. Asking parliament to ratify the contract would prolong the session, which Lauderdale, at least, was anxious to finish quickly so that he could get back to London to counter Middleton's intrigues. On September 10, in sending on the judges' opinion, he wrote Charles an extraordinary letter, by turns jovial, sardonic, impudent, and subservient. On 'the business of Buccleuch', he wrote, 'I knew well why you wrote to your Chancellor [Glencairn] about it . . . he was so roused by it & did so rant about it, that he will not join with us in any return, but thinks to do wonders'. In other words, Glencairn was in a panic and would not dream of venturing to join the judges in upholding their previous opinion. 'Be pleased to weight the whole & command what you please, & I need not tell you you shall be punctually obeyed. We durst not move what was *so positively illegal* [italics mine] without a clear order, but if it be your will you shall see we know no law but obedience.' This letter was very typical of Lauderdale. He made clear his distaste for the king's instructions, but if on reflection the king decided to go ahead, Lauderdale would carry out those instructions, law or no law.

Charles paused. When Moray began to make Gilmour's apologies for him, 'he stopped me, telling me that he . . . had not the least thought to his prejudice, but is most perfectly well satisfied with him'. This was a blow to Lady Wemyss, who hoped the king would fire him; she had detested Gilmour ever since he had told her in 1659 that Mary's 'pretended marriage', as he called it, was illegal. When Moray presented Charles with the legal opinions, Charles looked at them and then commanded Moray to speak. Moray put the case against any attempted ratification in the strongest possible terms. The judges, he said, thought the king's proposal legally unsound, and those he trusted with the weightiest matters of business there (i.e., Rothes and Lauderdale) were not supportive. A parliamentary act confirming the contract would be meaningless unless it was preceded by another act declaring that parliament had the power to dispose of the property of any subject without his consent and contrary to his declared will. Only thus could the act *salvo* be rendered null and Earl Francis's entail broken. Such an act would be contrary to the fundamental laws and practices of the kingdom. Moray added that all this was said not to 'sway him beyond what he thought fit'—which, of course, it was. But Moray rather spoiled the effect of his oratory by saying that he had prepared some drafts of statements Charles might send to parliament if he decided to go ahead anyway, including one dealing with the act *salvo*.

A few days later Moray had a different story to tell. Charles had received a dispatch from Glencairn which, he said, puzzled him. Glencairn kept insisting that without an act of parliament neither Monmouth nor Anna were secure in their estate, an attitude Moray had stigmatised to the king as making the judges look like fools or knaves, and Rothes and Lauderdale dishonest or disloyal. But Charles was sufficiently concerned to order Moray to consult with Clarendon. 'I could do nothing but submit, having already said to himself all I could upon the subject.' The involvement of English officialdom—not only Clarendon but also the king's brother and the English secretary of state, Sir Henry Bennet—was decisive. None of these men had any concern about the possible violation of Scots law involved in the ratification of the contract. All they cared about was that the king wanted it done: therefore it would come to pass.

The conclusive meeting took place on September 24, in Oxford—the court was on the road again, having spent a couple of weeks at Bath prior to coming to Oxford. Charles, his brother, Clarendon, and Bennet all listened to Moray's explanation of the contract. The king, said Moray, had been given bad advice, which, if followed, would reflect on his honour. He should listen to Gilmour—and he read Gilmour's letters. He carefully pointed out the differences between Scots and English law on the points under discussion. He defended Lauderdale's having referred the matter to Gilmour: Lauderdale was no lawyer. They must remember that Lady Wemyss did not trust Lauderdale—the implication being that she was unfairly criticising him. Moray might as well have saved his breath. The other three told Charles that he should go ahead. The best plan, they said, was to adjourn parliament and order Glencairn and various judges and lawyers to come to London to figure out how to proceed. Charles liked the idea. As he got up to go to supper, Moray took him aside and urged him not to adjourn parliament. This would not go down well in Scotland, said Moray, implying that it would look like English dictation. Charles was not convinced. So, while the king ate his supper, Moray repaired to the 'necessary room', found pen and paper, and drafted a statement for Charles to send to Commissioner Rothes instead of an order for adjournment. Charles read it over, said that he liked it, and would think about it until tomorrow. When tomorrow came, Charles postponed his decision for another day in order to go fox-hunting, which, he said, would make Lauderdale, no devotee of the chase, think he was as mad as other people. But now there was no turning back.

Charles returned from his day in the fields having decided to accept Moray's advice not to adjourn parliament. Instead the text of the act parliament was to pass would be prepared, and a set of instructions would be sent north with it. Secretary Bennet was instructed to draw up the necessary drafts. He shared them with Moray, who made counter-proposals. The king told them to confer, and they did, once again in the 'necessary room', a place with many uses. Of Moray's many proposed alterations in Bennet's text, only one of any importance was accepted. There was to be no statement that the act was the result of a royal command; rather, the king was acting on the advice of persons unspecified. This would save face if, as Moray thought possible, parliament balked at breaking an entail. On all other points Bennet's draft was preferred, evidently owing to Clarendon: Bennet himself was prepared to accept Moray's amendments. Clarendon, who cared nothing for Monmouth, seems to have acted as he did in order to create as much difficulty as possible for Lauderdale. At the final meeting, held late in the afternoon of September 27, Moray was kept waiting for an hour while the other four conferred; when he was finally called in, he gradually discovered that none of his suggested changes, other than the one already mentioned, was to be accepted. The principal change Moray wanted was that the estate revert to the next heir of entail with the title of duke of Buccleuch in the event that both Monmouth and Anna died childless. This, Moray argued, would make what he called the 'hard clause'—the breach of the entail—much more acceptable, since the breach would not be absolute, but rather would amount to the 'splendid adoption' of a new person into it.

Moray's failure meant that the provisions of the contract were not to be altered. The language of the act of confirmation was blunt: the contract violated the entail. This violation resulted from the initiative of 'the friends and curators of the said Duchess'—i.e., not the king, who for his part had created the dukedom and promised in the contract to provide the couple with lands valued at £40,000 sterling. Furthermore, the chief purpose of 'the irritant and resolutive clauses in the said tailzie' was to ensure that a female heir 'should not have power to marry at pleasure, but to the honor, dignity, and estate of Buccleuch'. Therefore, to prevent anyone from challenging the contract 'upon pretext of any irritant clause or provision mentioned in the foresaid band of tailzie . . . or any other pretext whatsoever', parliament ratified the entire contract, 'and especially that clause . . . whereby it is provided that failing of heirs of the Duchess' own body the said Duke and his heirs shall have right to the honor, dignity, and estate of Buccleuch in manner as is therein expressed'. The irritant clauses in the entail did not apply to this marriage contract. No Scottish court could ever even allow a challenge to be raised: the judges were forbidden 'in all time coming' to hear any plea based on the irritant clauses in Earl Francis's entail. The act *salvo* did not apply—and the one to be passed at the end of this parliament was to say so. As Moray commented, 'The business of *salvo jure* must not be minced'.

The instructions to be sent forward with this act caused as much trouble as the act itself. Charles, who watched everything very closely through a long Sunday in Oxford—he heard the first draft 'still not fully dressed' in the morning, and supper was on the table long before they finished—was concerned to stress the 'good and valuable' nature of the marriage contract, a phrase Moray disliked, and the great advantages it gave to the house of Buccleuch. The clauses irritant in the entail were clearly designed to prevent an heiress from marrying beneath her, and therefore did not apply. What the king wanted was 'not contrary to indispensable justice', a weaseling phrase if ever there was one. If the act did not pass, Rothes was authorised to prorogue parliament for a maximum of three months and order Glencairn, Lauderdale, Gilmour and the rest of the legal fraternity to get the contract through. If the act failed to pass, Charles would be 'not a little troubled to see ourself disappointed in a matter so nearly concerning our own honour as well as the good of the said Duke and Duchess, whom we so tenderly love'. Moray found this language not impossible as an expression of royal displeasure, though he would have preferred that Charles speak of how 'much concerned' he was that the ratification should pass. Finally, Charles ordered the unfavourable opinion of the court of session on the contract which he had received earlier in the month razed from the record, on the ground that it was irregularly arrived at.

This was 'a cloudy and knotty business', wrote Moray, but there was no way to stop it. Monmouth's people thought so too. 'Sir Robert Moray found us such work here, that although the King was fully . . . resolved to do the thing, yet Sir Robert's diligence to divert him from it, suspended it all the time we were at Bath,' wrote Thomas Ross, Monmouth's governor, to Wemyss, but at Oxford Clarendon, 'who hath taken a great deal of pains to effect all your desires', took things in hand. Moray's 'paper of advice how the act should be drawn' was rejected in favour of Clarendon's and Bennet's draft. Clarendon also 'made the King highly sensible of the cheat and abuse put upon him by those he trusted', meaning Gilmour, Rothes, and Lauderdale. 'We shall expect with impatience the issue, being confident, be it what it will, the authors of this trouble will, in time, repent it.' At the same time Ross wrote a crowing letter to Lady Wemyss, anticipating Gilmour's dismissal. 'Certainly the world will think it strange if he, that hath put so great an abuse upon his King, should continue President of his judicature. We have told all the stories we can find of him,' he went on, and asked Lady Wemyss for more ammunition if she had any. Alas for their hopes: Gilmour remained in his post.

If there was to be any parliamentary opposition to the confirmation, the initiative would have to come from Tweeddale, and everybody knew it. At the end of his immensely long letter to Lauderdale recounting the discussions of that Oxford Sunday—it covers eight pages in his tiny, spidery, difficult handwriting—Moray floated an idea that Lauderdale might think absurd, 'yet out it comes'. Tweeddale should support the act, if 'he could find it in his heart to do it'. He could get anything he wanted from the king if he did, and he would be doing a great service to his country, 'a more handsome sacrifice than the Roman did (I have forgot his name) that saved Rome by leaping into the Gap'. The 'service to his country' that Moray had in mind, given the nature of the act, was the preservation of Lauderdale's political career. His final word, at the end of his eight pages to the secretary, was that he and Rothes must get this act passed. Moray was on tenterhooks. On October 1 he wrote Lauderdale suggesting that, if there was trouble, an act might be drafted allowing for the breaking of an entail in favour of a royal child who married an heir with the consent of the curators. This would cover Monmouth's situation, but only Monmouth's, and prevent Tweeddale from getting support from other landowners. The proposed act, Moray went on, gave the members of parliament an admirable opportunity to show their loyalty and zeal by voting for it, since they would not be acting in response to a direct royal command.

Moray need not have worried. The end of the drama was anticlimax: on October 5, 1663, within a week of the king's sending his instructions, parliament ratified the marriage contract. There is no evidence of any debate, or any opposition. Lady Wemyss had triumphed. Her single-minded persistence had won out over the reluctance of the king, the opposition of the lawyers, and the foot-dragging of the politicians. It was perhaps the most remarkable of the many accomplishments of this extraordinary political manipulator and infighter. Walter Scott of Satchells, the family poet, who did not like her—he dedicated his poem, published in 1688, to Tweeddale's son—described her as

> . . . so impudent
> That she must always have her intent.

It is difficult to quarrel with that judgment.

At the end of November Lady Wemyss returned to her home with her annual pension of £500 sterling in her pocket, after a sad parting from her daughter. She had been in London almost a year and a half. She left behind her a crisp letter to Lauderdale complaining that her jointure had not been paid for two years because (for reasons not made clear in the letter) the bishop and dean of Edinburgh were in possession of the lands from which it was supposed to come. She wanted her money—as always, she wanted her money. It was an appropriate end to her custodianship of her daughter.

It is surprising that parliament's extraordinary action excited so little comment, both at the time and since. Never before had a Scottish parliament ratified the marriage contract of two of the king's subjects—it was an action unique in that body's long and variegated history. The implications of the enactment were frightening. At the king's behest—no one was deceived by the pretence that there was no royal initiative—parliament had ignored the law and trampled on a subject's property rights. If the king could do this by act of parliament, what else might he not do? The groundwork was laid for the erection of despotism by law, which Lauderdale was to consummate six years later. 'Never was king so absolute as you are in poor old Scotland,' he wrote to his master in November 1669, reporting parliament's passage of the Act of Supremacy of that year. The implications of the legislation of 1669 were not lost on members of parliament in England, where Lauderdale became a sinister and detested figure. But what parliament had done in 1663 was generally ignored in both countries. Perhaps the case was thought to be unique because the king's son was involved. No one else's rights would be at risk; only Lady Jean and her descendants would suffer. It was as though there was a conspiracy of silence—a silence shared by the victims themselves.

Tweeddale had done nothing. What Lauderdale may have said to him is unknown. After all the many letters of September there is nothing on the marriage contract in the extant Lauderdale correspondence after October 1, not even the letter to the king announcing parliament's action, although presumably Lauderdale wrote one. Contemporary observers were no wiser. 'How far it [the ratification] may import as to some who have been silent to it,' wrote one of Haychesters' correspondents the next day, 'I confess with me is a mystery of State, which, in its own time, may be visible and evident.' Haychesters' own bitter gloss was that what the king promised Tweeddale 'is not well known nor safe to be inquired into'.

Why did Tweeddale behave as he did? Bishop Burnet, who knew him well and otherwise thought highly of him, was very critical:

his 'compliance . . . brought a great cloud upon him'. But in another place in his history Burnet put his finger on Tweeddale's motivation. Tweeddale, 'though his children were the next heirs, who by this were robbed of their right, had yet given way to it in so frank a manner that the king was enough inclined both to oblige and to trust him'. In fact Tweeddale had little choice. Given the king's personal stake in the ratification, resistance to his wishes would have been both vain and counterproductive. Tweeddale knew that the only possible way to recover what his wife and children had lost was with the approval, or at least the acquiescence, of the king. He had not given up—far from it. He had made no trouble in parliament, but when the formal votes were taken on the last day of the session, he was not there. He had dropped out of the procession on its way to the parliament house, and had spent the time in the house of a goldsmith named Alexander Reid, in the company of other witnesses, whose testimony to that effect was carefully notarised. This was proof, if he should need it, that he had not voted to confirm the marriage contract. But his precautions were taken very quietly, and passed unnoticed.

Prior to October 1663 Charles had no reason to look with favour upon Tweeddale, the ex-Cromwellian who had not wanted to see James Guthrie executed. But now he had. He was, wrote Haychesters, convinced, now, that Tweeddale was an honest man. When Tweeddale went to London in January 1664, Lauderdale took him 'in his riding posture' to the king, who, wrote Lauderdale, 'gave him as kind a reception as I think he could desire'. In February Charles did what Moray in the previous September had suggested he do, and put Lady Tweeddale back in line for the estate. If both Anna and Monmouth died without children, she and her heirs would have it, as an earldom. It seems very likely that Lauderdale was behind the king's action, though there is no direct proof. It was a gesture that cost Monmouth nothing, allowed the Tweeddales to hope that the great prize might yet be theirs, and made a firm political ally for the secretary of this cousin of his, an intelligent, experienced, and potentially very useful man.

For a time it appeared that Tweeddale had judged the situation correctly. His alliance with Lauderdale was further cemented in 1666, when his eldest son, Lord Yester, the disappointed candidate for Mary's and then Anna's hand, married Lauderdale's daughter, his only child. For Tweeddale it was potentially a wonderfully

profitable marriage. The second son of the young couple would inherit the Lauderdale estates. And the immensely influential secretary
now had a direct interest in the future of the Buccleuch inheritance.
In 1671, while she was still childless, Anna remarked to her former
brother-in-law Tarras 'with a disdainful smile, "Somebody asked
my Lord Lauderdale who would succeed to my estate if I had no children, and he answered, who but his grandchild my Lord Yester's
son"'.

Tweeddale's political career flourished. For four years, from 1667
to 1671, he was Lauderdale's chief collaborator in the government in
Edinburgh. During those years, with Lauderdale's help, he nego-
tiated a very favourable settlement of his obligations to the Buccleuch estate. His debt, which had stood at over £65,000 in 1664,
was recalculated at £15,600 in 1667 thanks to two counterclaims he
and Lady Jean put forward. But in 1671 his relationship with Lauderdale began to sour. There were political disagreements, but what
brought about the permanent breach between the two was a savage
family quarrel. In December 1671 Lauderdale's estranged wife died
in Paris. She left her property, including the family jewels, to her
daughter Lady Yester. Lauderdale wanted it all, for himself and his
intended new wife, whom he married as soon as he decently could,
and he got it, through a combination of political influence, lying,
and chicanery. He and Tweeddale quarreled irrevocably. Lauderdale
took his daughter to court, disinherited his grandson, making his
brother the heir to his titles and estates, and refused to see his grandchildren any more.* Tweeddale went into open political opposition, and in June 1674 lost all his government offices. In that same
month, in what was by no means a coincidence, the duke and duchess
of Monmouth, having come of age, repudiated the settlement made
in their name in 1667 and demanded that Tweeddale pay the full
amount of the debt. The dispute dragged on for five years. Toward
the end Tweeddale in desperation appealed to Anna to be merciful,
talking of the welfare of the family and how fond her father had been
of Lady Jean. The duchess was not moved. She would not be 'unnatural to my kindred', she wrote to a friend, but she would not 'be persuaded to live in debt and miserably all my life to please him'.

---

* Tweeddale's embittered account of his family's quarrel with Lauderdale can be
found, in several versions, in his papers in the National Library of Scotland. It is
too long a tale to tell here; I hope to tell it elsewhere.

Tweeddale had to pay. By the time the final settlement was reached in 1679, Tweeddale's debt stood at £111,853 15 shillings, of which over £67,000 was interest. He was allowed a total of £49,453 15 shillings, for the two counterclaims against the estate. So he owed £62,400. In return the Monmouths granted him what he must have regarded as a non-existent boon. In 1680 the court of session formally nullified those clauses in Anna's marriage contract, the parliamentary ratification of 1663, and the subsequent regrants of the Buccleuch estate that violated Earl Francis's entail. Anna and Monmouth were the parents of three apparently healthy children; so it was safe to restore Lady Jean to her place in the succession to the great estate. The clause irritant was at long last laid to rest; Tweeddale's hope that at some future time he might be able to strike at Duchess Anna in court vanished forever.

Once the settlement was made, Tweeddale tried appealing to the king for relief, and got nowhere. By June 1680 he had actually paid £20,000, almost one third of what he owed. Monmouth's fall from grace with his father occasioned another fruitless appeal in 1682. The duke's rebellion, forfeiture, and death in 1685 produced no benefit either; King James saw no reason to provide relief to Tweeddale at the expense of his friend Duchess Anna. In April 1688 Tweeddale finally gave up. He sold his ancestral lands in Tweeddale to the duke of Queensberry for over £350,000. The final payment on his debt to the house of Buccleuch was made in 1690. The last instalment came to £18,087 5s 4d; with interest, the £62,400 of 1679 had swollen to over £71,000. A long, long story was over.

Tweeddale lived for seven years after that final payment. In the reign of William III his political fortunes revived. He was lord chancellor for four years, and received a marquisate. King William also renewed the lease of the lordship and regality of Dunfermline, a valuable piece of crown property which Tweeddale had acquired from the previous lessee, his extravagant Uncle Charles, the first cause of his financial woes. It was a welcome piece of royal generosity. He died in 1697, aged seventy-one. One person's hostility never varied. 'My daughter Dalkeith [the wife of Anna's eldest son] is very near her time,' wrote Anna to the earl of Cromartie in October 1694, 'to comfort my friend Tweeddale in his old age.' There would be one more life between Tweeddale's family and the Buccleuch estate. To the very end, after all the money had been paid and all questions about the entail resolved, Tweeddale remained for Anna what he had always been: the wicked uncle.

7

Wife to Prince Perkin

S ir Walter Scott's Last Minstrel, 'scorn'd and poor', who 'begg'd
his bread from door to door', received a kindly welcome from
the ageing duchess of Buccleuch when he ventured past her portal,

> For she had known adversity,
> Though born in such a high degree;
> In pride of power, in beauty's bloom,
> Had wept o'er Monmouth's bloody tomb!

Anna may have broken down at her last meeting with her husband (see above, p.2), but it is unlikely that she shed many tears at his grave. It is true that Matthew Prior wrote about 'the sad beauties of fair Annabel,' and that in February 1686 John Evelyn wrote that she 'being in the same seat with me [at the church of St. Martin's in the Fields] appeared with a very sad and afflicted countenance', but this may have been due to the as-yet unresolved disposition of the Buccleuch estate rather than to grief. Her marriage had failed long before the executioner formally ended it, and so had all pretence about it.

Monmouth's career as one of the court's playboys began early. Pepys, who described him in a not-unfriendly way in July 1665 as 'the most skittish leaping gallant that ever I saw', by December 1666 wrote that he spent his time viciously and idly. In June 1667, when the rumour was abroad that Monmouth would go to France as a tourist, Pepys wrote that such a visit 'will become him much more than to live whoring and rogueing of it here as he now does'. To be sure, such conduct was far from unusual at Charles II's court. Indeed, serious-minded men who did not sleep around, such as Secretary of State Arlington, were thought of as stuffy and tedious, and were the butt of the jokes of the so-called 'court wits'. But Monmouth went further. In 1674 he took up with Eleanor Needham, set her up in a house in what is now Great Russell Street, and over the next six years fathered four children by her. Then, in 1680, when he was thirty-one, he fell in love, genuinely in love, with Lady Henrietta Wentworth, an attractive twenty-year-old. Their love was mutual and passionate, and it lasted. Monmouth regarded her as his real wife, and went to his death with her name on his lips. Henrietta had shared his troubles and his exile, and his death broke her heart. She died nine months later, in April 1686.

What went wrong with Anna's marriage? Why did it not work at least well enough to preserve appearances and allow her to save face? The evidence all points to Monmouth as the guiltier party. Monmouth has been the subject of a lot of books because of his great position, his crucial role in the political crisis that followed the eruption of the Popish Plot, and his leadership of the futile rebellion that brought him to the block. But at bottom he was not a very interesting young man. His assets, apart from his parentage, were his dazzling good looks, his great charm and affability, his undoubted courage, his generosity, as a military officer his kindness to and concern for his soldiers, and his straightforwardness. But his weaknesses were fatal. He was immensely unintelligent and not very well informed. He was limitlessly self-indulgent: what he wanted he reached for, without consideration for others. Above all, he was pliable. Stronger and more intelligent men could make use of him for their own purposes, as the earl of Shaftesbury did during the exclusion crisis. He was, wrote the earl of Ailesbury, 'a weak person . . . led astray by enthusiastic villains'. So obvious was it, as Ailesbury put it, that he could be 'led by the nose', even 'by lewd and beggarly fellows of no religion or morals', that there were those who believed that his ambition to wear a crown was Anna's doing. Henry Sidney, who did not admire her, wrote of the 'pretentions that he had in his head, which he hath been put on by his wife'. In a note Sidney added that 'She governed the Duke [of York] and made him do several things for her husband which he repents of'. Sidney had it wrong. The one person close to Monmouth who had no influence over his behaviour was his wife.

Anna was not a warm person. She grew into a chilly and rather flinty woman, who in later years said of herself that there were few people she loved very much. 'All the world are for themselves,' she wrote to the earl of Cromartie in 1712, 'so I am for me.' One of Monmouth's biographers calls her 'repellingly righteous'. But this is unnecessarily harsh. Sir Stephen Fox, who knew her well because of both his long involvement in her financial affairs as the London agent of the various managers of her estates and her marriage in 1688 to Lord Cornwallis, his daughter's widower, found her personality unstable, subject to fits of penitence, despair, and rage. Like her mother, Anna was tough and combative. 'I cannot brag of being very well yet,' she once wrote to her nephew after receiving what she regarded as an insult to his father and herself, 'but I will do what I can to be so, to lay about me amongst my enemies'—people such as Tweeddale. The most quoted description of Anna is that of John Evelyn, written in 1673 after he had dined with her and Monmouth at Lord Arlington's: 'certainly one of the wisest and craftiest of her sex: she has much wit'. Not unflattering, but hardly enthusiastic. Henry Sidney, while admitting the wit—'very assuming and witty', he called her—went on to say that 'she hath little sincerity'. No one else wrote that, and Evelyn, at the time of Monmouth's execution, described her as 'a virtuous and excellent lady'. Monmouth, on the other hand, wrote Evelyn, was 'of an easy nature, debauched by lust, seduced by crafty knaves'. He was indeed what Nell Gwyn called him—and the label gained instant currency—Prince Perkin.*

Anna may have resembled her mother in a number of ways, but it is difficult to avoid the conclusion that it was the early years of her married life, her adolescence, that formed her character. In 1663 she was still a child, writing sad little notes to her stepfather, wishing her mother would stay with her longer. Here is one, dated September 22, 1663, in its entirety, bad spelling included (like her uncle Rothes she was an atrocious speller):

> I could not bot let you know of ane verie fine galant I have gotn sene the Duke want with the King, to carie me to the play. It is my brother Elho [Lord Elcho, the Wemyss's son, a boy of eight]. Hi dos love them verie well, and verie oft wi do wish your Lordship with ous. Remember my serves to my sistr Lady Margrat, and ever estim me, my Lord, your Lordship's most obedent daughtr,
>
> > Anna Buccleuch
>
> I do wish your Lordship war hir, that you might kep my Lady with me all thes wenter, for shi dos intend to go much to soun.

---

* Perkin Warbeck, the pretender to Henry VII's throne, claimed to be Prince Richard, duke of York.

But Lady Wemyss did go home, and Anna was left to grow up virtually by herself (though she did briefly have a governess) in Charles's raffish court, along with her skittish, leaping gallant and his tutor, Thomas Ross, who stayed with Monmouth until his death in 1675. Ross was a Scot who had been with Monmouth since before the Restoration and who was now, formally, the keeper of the king's libraries. He was an indulgent tutor, who provided his pupil with so little training that at fifteen Monmouth found it difficult to write a letter, even to his father. That chore, Ross commented, made the 'poor Duke sigh and sweat, not being used to write'. Ross had much influence over Monmouth, not all of it good. The compilation known as the memoirs of James II declares that it was Ross who first persuaded Monmouth that Charles really had married his mother, Lucy Walter, that 'beautiful strumpet', as Evelyn called her. (Rumour, said Pepys, described her as a common whore.) Almost as soon as Monmouth arrived in England the story that he was legitimate began to circulate. By February 1664 Pepys was reporting that Monmouth—not yet fifteen—was threatening to kill anyone who denied it.

Charles himself helped give such rumours credence. He told Monmouth to put his hat on when dancing with Queen Catherine, a privilege of royalty. Monmouth wore purple when the court went into mourning for the late duke of Savoy, another privilege of royalty. This, wrote Pepys, 'gives great offense', and the duke of York was understandably unhappy. These were foolish gestures on Charles's part, springing from the love he had for his beautiful boy. The fact of the matter is that the person most responsible for the failure of Monmouth's and Anna's marriage was King Charles himself. As Pepys observed, he doted on Monmouth 'beyond measure', and spoiled him by denying him nothing. There was money, money in profusion, money whenever it was wanted. The two children spent with no sense of discipline at all, and they both became hopelessly extravagant. After Lady Wemyss went back to Scotland in November 1663, the servants and the bills went unpaid, and the debts mounted up, to the point where Monmouth was formally summoned to appear in court because he had not paid the £300* he owed for the paving of Hedge Lane, where they lived when they were not in residence at court. Late in 1666 Tweeddale, who as one of

* All the monetary figures given in this chapter are in pounds sterling.

Monmouth's curators was well informed, estimated the debt at £25,000. One of the chief responsibilities of a committee Charles appointed at the beginning of 1665 to advise him on the young couple's affairs was to restore order to their finances. This did not happen until the end of the year, when Sir Stephen Fox replaced Alderman Backwell as the receiver of the income from the Buccleuch estates and took their affairs in hand. One of his first acts was to lend them £500 for Anna's 'necessarys' and to pay for their move from Oxford to London, along with the rest of the court, after the plague subsided. A balance sheet of 1666 listed the servants' wages, board, and liveries at £3,500 and the stables at £1,135 more; the duke's and duchess's allowance for clothes and pocket money was set at £1,200 each per year. This was fantasy. In 1671 Anna spent £1,200, almost a quarter of a million pounds in today's money, on a pair of diamond earrings. The stables by then were costing over £1,800 a year, and their total expenses, not counting such items as the earrings, were running at about £12,000 a year, more than the total Buccleuch rent roll, which was around £10,000.

The money for the young couple's extravagant lifestyle came from the king. A few months after his beloved son arrived in England Charles granted the lad of thirteen the right to license white cloth for export, for which his deputy paid him £8,000 a year. In February 1665, when Monmouth and Anna began to cohabit, there was a pension of £6,000 a year. The king raised it to £8,000 in 1672 with the birth of the couple's first son, with a reversion of £4,000 each to Anna and the boy should Monmouth predecease them. As the family grew, so did the king's largesse. By 1677 there was an extra £1,600 a year for Charles's grandchildren, of whom there were then three.

The royal gifts did not stop there. There were jewels and plate and land, money for coaches and horses and travel. There was housing, and money for its maintenance: the Hedge Lane house in London, an eleven-room suite in the palace of Whitehall, a country house in Chiswick, and, when that turned out not to please them, a far more expensive one at Moor Park, near Rickmansworth in Hertfordshire. Anna came to love Moor Park; she spent a great deal of time there as her relations with her husband soured. Offices rained down on Monmouth, especially after he came of age: captain of the guard, master of the horse, chief justice in eyre south of the Trent, two lord-lieutenancies, and, rather oddly, the chancellorship of

Cambridge University in 1674.* From time to time there were casual gifts of money, and in 1667 a huge advance on his pension to help clear off his and Anna's debts. The golden stream was unceasing. An accounting made in 1681 by Will Chiffinch, whom David Ogg describes as the king's 'confidential agent, procurer-general, and pawnbroker-in-chief', indicates that in 1672 and 1673 alone Monmouth received a total of £43,000, including a special gift of £5,000 to celebrate Anna's lying-in in 1672. Even after Monmouth defied his father and fell out with him, the stream did not dry up altogether. As late as December 1684 payments of pension money were still being made.

Monmouth's appointment as captain of the king's guards in 1668 indicated that Charles had made up his mind about his son's future: he was to be a soldier. This was a suitable career for a royal bastard. There is no evidence that Charles ever for a moment entertained the idea of making Monmouth his heir, fond though he was of the boy: the principle of indefeasible hereditary right, so crucial to the fortunes of the Stewart dynasty, could not be so breached. Charles sent the young duke to sea with his uncle James, the Lord Admiral, at the beginning of the Dutch war, and he was on the flagship during the bloody victory at Southwold Bay in June 1665. He showed his courage, and won his uncle's praise, but the battle had been personally too costly for his father. Charles's and York's intimate friend, Charles Berkeley, earl of Falmouth, standing next to York on the quarterdeck, was killed; his blood spattered all over York. This was too close a call: Charles kept his boy at court, out of harm's way, for the rest of the war. The navy was York's province; so Charles groomed Monmouth for the army. He performed well—he looked after his regiments in French service during the Dutch war of the 1670s, he displayed conspicuous bravery at the siege of Maastricht in 1673, and, at the beginning of his disastrous political adventure, he put down the rebellion in southwest Scotland in 1679 easily and, ignoring advice to the contrary, showed mercy to the defeated rebels. Monmouth had the makings of a good soldier. Under other circumstances his career might have resembled that of that other royal bastard, his first cousin the duke of Berwick. But it was not to be.

---

* From the racetrack at Newmarket that year Monmouth wrote to the vice-chancellor of Cambridge with orders that divinity students were to cut their hair and that in future preachers were not to read their sermons but deliver them from memory. One wonders whose ideas these were.

Because Monmouth was spoiled. It was all too easy: the money, the luxuries, the assured position, the deference. Not only did the king dote on him, so did everybody else, especially the women, even that case-hardened old battleaxe Lady Wemyss.* Monmouth had the charisma of his great-great-grandmother Mary Queen of Scots. He was well aware of his capacity to charm, and, like her, he came to depend on it to get him out of the difficulties into which his feckless-ness led him. For a long time it did, because he could always count on the one person whose love for him never ceased, his father. When Charles II died the sands ran out very quickly.

At court Monmouth fell in with an older crowd, the 'fast' crowd, the court rakehells whose most prominent member was the duke of Buckingham, that charming, witty chameleon who, as Dryden said, was everything by starts and nothing long. A man who would kill his mistress's husband in a duel, move the lady into his town house, and send his wife home to her father when she protested, was hardly an ideal role model for an adolescent of unformed charac-ter. It was a deceptively attractive crowd, witty and amusing; they stood well with the king, who also was witty and amusing and en-joyed his courtiers' japes. Buckingham had been the king's friend from childhood, and was at Worcester with him, which helps to ex-plain Charles's tolerance of the duke's frequently outrageous perso-nal and political behaviour. No king ever stood less upon his dignity than Charles. Even the earl of Rochester, whose lampooning of the king was frequently obscene, and who wrote the two most fa-mous lines about Charles ever penned—

> Restless he rolls about from whore to whore,
> A Merry Monarch, scandalous and poor

—earned no more than occasional stretches of banishment from court for his audacity. (These were no doubt therapeutic, as they required the peccant poet to live in the country with his wife, and,

---

* When she heard of Monmouth's defeat at Sedgemoor, Lady Wemyss's daughter Margaret, now countess of Wemyss in her own right, wrote to her nephew, Lord Melville's son—Melville was in exile—'I was unwilling to write to my sister [Catherine Melville, Lady Wemyss's daughter by her first husband] lest she knew not of it; but if her business be not very pressing, I think she should come here and wait on our dear mother, who does not yet believe him in such hazard. Alas, the sad stroke will be heavy enough when it comes, without the aggravation of groundless hopes. The Lord comfort her. I am in such confusion I can write no more'.

perhaps, sober up from time to time.) Charles himself supplied copy for the satirists. When his adolescent son first came to court he was beginning his fruitless and very public pursuit of the beautiful Frances Stuart, to the equally public irritation of his reigning mistress, the bad-tempered Castlemaine, and his life continued so. In December 1677 Rochester's friend Henry Savile wrote to him of a troop of French comedians who had recently been performing at Whitehall 'so very well that it is a thousand pities they should not stay, especially a young wench of fifteen' of great beauty and sweetness. 'It were a shame to the nation that she should carry away a maidenhead she pretends to have brought and that nobody here has either wit or address or money enough to go to the price of. The King sighs and despairs and says nobody but Sir George Downing or my Lord Ranelagh can possibly purchase her.'[*] As the duke of Buckingham, no mean poet himself though not in Rochester's class, put it in a lampoon of the king:

> Look over all the Universal Frame,
> There's not a thing the Will of Man can name
> In which this Ugly, perjur'd Rogue delights,
> But Ducks and loytering, butter'd Buns and whites.[†]

Such a man was not a role model for Monmouth either.

So Monmouth adopted the court's fashionable vices. At first there was merely drinking and gambling, but the whoring followed soon enough. A Tuscan visitor to Charles's court in 1667–68 remarked that Monmouth, whom he called 'weak and ignorant', had already had several bouts of venereal disease. There were public scrapes. Monmouth was commonly held responsible for the vicious attack on Sir John Coventry in 1670. Coventry was a member of parliament who proposed a tax on theatregoers. In the course of the debate he made an incautious reference to the king's fondness for actresses—Nell Gwyn, as everyone knew, was Charles's current enthusiasm. Coventry's reward was to be set upon late one night as he was returning from a tavern and have his nose slit to the bone. The attackers were members of Monmouth's troop of guards, who went to

---

[*] Downing and Ranelagh were both very wealthy men who had profited from treasury posts, Downing's in England, Ranelagh's in Ireland. Downing also did well in real estate.

[†] 'Butter'd buns' are prostitutes; 'whites', silver money.

Monmouth's house in Hedge Lane to report their success. Worse was to follow. In February 1671 Monmouth and two other dukes, Somerset and Monck's son Albemarle, went to Whetstone Park, a lane north of Lincoln's Inn Fields, to get drunk and look for whores. They created a disturbance and murdered a beadle who tried to investigate. This behaviour required a royal pardon, which was duly given: boys will be boys. Like both his parents, Monmouth had an apparently insatiable sexual appetite, and his behaviour was less than discreet. His fellow roisterer Albemarle thought it wise to take his wife to the country, out of temptation's way. When Monmouth visited France in 1668 his flirtatious behaviour with his aunt Henrietta, only five years his senior, provoked the venomous jealousy of her loathsome husband, the duc d'Orléans.

What did Anna have to offer to this dazzling, spoiled child of fortune? What was her attraction for him? Money, of course. She was not beautiful by Restoration standards: she did not resemble the sloe-eyed, lush beauties who, in their eye-catching décolletage, gaze vacantly at us from Lely's canvases. She was, by all accounts, lively and intelligent, but these were not characteristics that made a woman pleasing to Monmouth. She found her husband's interest in astrology and enthusiasm for fortune tellers ridiculous, and poked fun at him for his credulity.* Monmouth, on the other hand, complained that Anna was not a good manager. 'Pray let me know if my wife begins to look after her business at home,' he wrote from Brussels in 1677 to Lord Melville, the principal manager of her Scottish estates, 'and if there be any hopes of her being a good housewife.' They both liked the theatre, Monmouth rather tepidly, Anna with genuine enthusiasm—it was fashionable to like the theatre, since the king was such a keen and frequent playgoer. They were not really very compatible.

One passion they did share. They both loved to dance, and they were both very good at it. Pepys praised Anna's dancing the first time he saw her perform, when she was only eleven; Monmouth was famously good. He danced even better than his father, no mean feat. In France in 1668 he taught his aunt Henrietta, also a beautiful dancer, various English country dances, which helped provoke her

---

* Monmouth while in France in 1668 was much taken with the Abbé Pregnani, who cast a horoscope for him. The abbé came to England in 1669, where, to Charles's amusement, he consistently picked the wrong horses at Newmarket, costing Monmouth quite a lot of money.

husband's jealousy. Perhaps this shared enthusiasm might have forged a bond between Monmouth and Anna; it was just about all they had in common. Then, with sad and sudden finality, the potential bond was destroyed. On May 8, 1668, while dancing at her lodgings, Anna fell and injured herself badly. Pepys's information, reported the following day, was that she had sprained her hip, but it was far more serious than that. The hip was dislocated. Let the king tell the story, in his letter to his sister on May 14: 'I have been in great trouble for James his wife, her thigh being as we thought set very well, for three days together. At last we found it was still out, so that the day before yesterday it was set with all the torture imaginable; she is now pretty well, and I hope will not be lame'. Alas for the king's—and Anna's—hopes. As Pepys wrote on July 15, she 'is still lame and likely always to be so—which is a sad chance for a young [lady] to get, only by trying of tricks in dancing'. His gloomier report, on September 20, that 'her lame leg . . . is likely to grow shorter and shorter', happily turned out not to be true. But she limped for the rest of her life. Her career as a famous dancer was over. She was just seventeen.

Anna was brave and determined. In July she went to Bath to recuperate, and spent the better part of two months there. The baths did not help, though she was reported to be in good spirits, and by the first of September felt well enough to pay an unannounced visit to Bristol before returning to Whitehall. Inevitably, she faced the question of a new operation to reset the hip, and shied away from the pain. She 'has the courage only to resolve to have her hip set but not to suffer it to be done', wrote one court lady in January 1669, 'when she goes about it, makes little trials, and then begs of them to let her alone'. She would live with her infirmity.

Where was Anna's husband during all this? For the most part, elsewhere. He had returned from France in April 1668, but apparently he was not present when Anna had her accident. He went to France again in June with a confidential message from Charles to Henrietta which helped set in train the negotiations that led to the secret treaty of Dover in 1670. He returned to England in July but was in no hurry to visit his convalescent wife at Bath, nor did his father push him to do so. On August 15 the king, York, and Monmouth had an agreeable outing on the Thames pursuing wildfowl. Finally, in late August, Monmouth made a quick trip to Bath, found Anna 'pretty well recovered', and hurried back to London to prepare for the elaborate ceremony which marked his assumption of the command of the king's guard. Anna's presence on this occasion was not reported, but no doubt she was there. She was well enough to accompany the court to Suffolk in the autumn; she and Queen Catherine stayed at Audley End, which the king was in the process of purchasing, while their husbands went on to Newmarket.

It is difficult to overestimate the impact of this accident on Anna's marriage. To be maimed for life at seventeen was bad enough. To have the mishap wipe out the only bond she had with her husband as well as two of her greatest pleasures—she loved to act as well as dance—was even worse. Monmouth had given no particular indication that he cared much for her before this; he now turned away completely. One of the questions he put to the Abbé Pregnani in early 1669, along with the names of the Newmarket winners, was whether he, his father, or his uncle would be the first to bed down a lady named Elizabeth Waller, who had caught his eye. When the children were born he behaved correctly. He returned from France in August 1672 to be present at Anna's first lying-in and was described by a foreign observer as being 'friend now again with his wife'. Two years later he grieved when the little boy died, as did his aunt by marriage Lady Jean Tweeddale, now locked in a bitter lawsuit with her niece (see above, p. 94). 'I pray God comfort his mother under so sad an affliction,' she wrote. Lady Jean was a kindly woman, who rejoiced in Anna's successful delivery of a new son later that year, even though the boy's existence hurt her chances of inheriting the Buccleuch fortune. That sort of kindness was foreign to Anna's nature by now, and small wonder. Monmouth's infidelities grieved her deeply, and embittered her. When she learned of Monmouth's liaison with Eleanor Needham, she 'does take it mightily to heart,' wrote her friend, young Princess Mary. Whether this was genuine love or merely hurt pride is impossible to say. Anna maintained her stoic front. Henceforth she treated Monmouth with chilly and distant respect, calling him 'Sir' when he returned from his victorious campaign in Scotland in 1679. But she never emulated him: she did not sleep around. Contemporary descriptions of Anna use the adjective 'virtuous', one not often applied to the ladies of Charles's court.

Charles's Whitehall was a difficult place for a woman like Anna. In some ways it resembled that of his grandfather James I. Both kings disliked ceremony, had irregular working habits, and were bored by routine. Both had grown up in, and become accustomed to, an atmosphere of informality, Charles in his penurious exile, James in his almost equally penurious court in Scotland. In consequence both were open-handed with their friends, their courtiers, and those they loved when they came to their promised land. The accession of each to the English throne put an end to a long period of strain, uncertainty, and turmoil, and inaugurated a postwar atmosphere of relaxation and pleasure-seeking which neither did anything to check. Neither had a routine, save for Charles's daily public dinner in the Banqueting Hall, neither cared for the drudgery of government or the drudges who performed it, the Salisburys and the Clarendons. James preferred the company of intellectuals, especially theologians like Lancelot Andrewes, and handsome young men like his Buckingham; Charles the company of wits like his Buckingham, and pretty, acquiescent young women. Their favourites were expensive, and influential in questions of patronage, though not until the end, with James's Buckingham and Charles's Louise de Kéroualle, were they perceived as playing a major political role.

There were differences. Charles and those around him never forgot that they were returned émigrés. Beneath the hectic gaiety and license of Restoration Whitehall there was an undercurrent of fear that somehow, some time, the adherents of the Good Old Cause might try again, in England or Scotland or both. Hysteria was always present, just below the surface of English life; hence the reaction to the fictions of Titus Oates. No such phenomenon existed in Jacobean England, as witness the measured response to the very real danger represented by Guy Fawkes and his fellow-conspirators. Charles liked London, and by preference spent most of his time there; James disliked the city and spent as much time as he could at places like Royston, where he could indulge his passion for the chase. James's court may have been squalid, raffish, drunken, and disorganised, but the king never publicly condoned vice and moved promptly in such matters as the murder of Sir Thomas Overbury. At Charles's court there was no effort to cover up the vice, the sexual license, and the brutal behaviour of courtiers—it was the Commons, not the king, who reacted with horror to the cowardly attack on Sir John Coventry.

Charles's was a male-dominated court where, beneath the surface politeness, women were regarded as sexual playthings—an uncomfortable place for any woman unwilling to play the strumpet. Some could not cope with it. The beautiful Frances Stuart was driven to elopement to get away from the king's unwelcome attentions. John Evelyn's pious friend Margaret Blagge abandoned her position as a maid of honour and simply fled. Maids of honour were in a very difficult position. They had little to occupy their time, it was difficult to find a husband there (except, of course, someone else's), and courtiers regarded them as fair game. There was much fine talk about 'the ladies', but no man took them seriously as people. Only once did the court ladies revolt: they bitterly protested at the portrayal of upper-class women as lascivious hypocrites in *The Country Wife*. The general male reaction was surprise. Wycherley, after all, was only saying in elegant language what the earl of Rochester, who wrote a lot of dirty poetry, said more concisely about that symbol of Charles's court, Lady Castlemaine, now duchess of Cleveland:

> Quoth the Duchess of Cl————to Mrs. Kn————,
> I'd fain have a prick, but how to come by't;
> I desire you'll be secret, and give your advice,
> Though cunt be not coy, reputation is nice.

Anna was, of course, a special sort of court lady. She was a member of the royal family, and since, unlike Anne Hyde, the first duchess of York, she gave the court wits no opening to attack her sexual behaviour, the poets and the gossips forebore to mention her in their reports of the steamy goings-on in the bedrooms of the great. She got on well with the royal brothers, who liked her very much. She was a lady of Queen Catherine's bedchamber, and her friend: they had much in common, as the neglected wives of philandering husbands.* There is no evidence as to her relations with Anne Hyde, but she was friendly with York's second wife, Mary of Modena, another lonely royal lady, and very close to young Princess Mary. She helped to 'undress' the unhappy young girl of fifteen at her marriage to the future William III, and accompanied Mary of Modena when she visited Mary in the Netherlands shortly thereafter.

One would not expect Anna to have much impact on a court such as Charles's, and she did not. Things might have been different had

---

* In 1670, during the court's autumnal pilgrimage to Suffolk for the Newmarket races, the queen was reported to have ridden to Newport, near Audley End where the ladies were staying, to buy a pair of stockings for 'her sweet heart the Duchess of Monmouth'.

she not suffered her accident, which ended her career as an amateur actress. Restoration theatre was a new and marvellous world, with its previously unthinkable innovation, women in women's parts. The king loved it; it was fashionable; there were quantities of playwrights. But by contrast with the years before the civil war, when the masque flourished at the courts of the king's father and grandfather, with the ladies and gentlemen of the court constituting the cast, there were no 'amateur' productions given at Charles's court until January 13, 1668. On that occasion Dryden's *The Indian Emperor* was performed, and it is not far-fetched to conclude that Anna was responsible. The play had first been performed in 1665. In October 1667 Dryden published the text with a fulsome dedication to Anna, praising her beauty, virtue, and generosity. 'Tis so much your inclination to do good, that you stay not to be asked.' Four months later it was played at court, with Anna and Monmouth in the cast. Pepys reported that none of the women could act at all except Anna and Mrs. Cornwallis, who were both very good. A few weeks later a translation of Corneille's *Horace* was put on, with Anna again in the cast. The focus of attention on that occasion was Lady Castlemaine, who, said Evelyn, covered herself with jewellery worth £40,000. Then came Anna's accident, and we hear no more about her appearances on the stage. According to Eleanore Boswell, the historian of the Restoration court stage, the phenomenon of amateur productions at court was shortlived: *The Indian Emperor* was the first, and *Calisto*, in 1674, the last. *Calisto* had an all-female cast, made up of maids of honour and the Princesses Mary and Anne, but not Anna, although some of the rehearsals took place at her lodgings. Had Anna not been lamed, amateur productions at court might have had a much longer life.

Anna was seriously interested in the arts. Dryden, who dedicated his works to all and sundry, including Monmouth, in his later years described her as his 'first and best patroness'. This was not literally true—she was not his first—but she was crucial to his career. She admired his poetry, and she helped him with the managers of commercial theatres. He, in turn, praised her in his work. She was the 'charming Annabel' in his great polemic against Absalom her husband;* she was the loyal and faithful Marmoutière in *The Duke of Guise*, who urges Guise (Monmouth) not to defy his king and behave

* Anna is the only person mentioned in *Absalom and Achitophel* who does not have a Biblical name, perhaps because the Biblical Absalom was unmarried.

more moderately. Her friendship was invaluable to Dryden after 1688, when Dryden the Tory-turned-Catholic might otherwise have been in very bad odour. In 1691 he sent the text of *King Arthur*, which he wrote in collaboration with William Purcell, to her. Anna recommended it to her friend Queen Mary, and Dryden's career was saved by the 'excellent Duchess, the patroness of my poor unworthy poetry', as he had called her eight years before. Dryden was not the only writer who thus praised her. Thomas Shadwell, who hated Dryden, described her as

> The best patroness of wit and stage,
> The joy, the pride, the wonder of the age,

in excoriating Dryden for repaying her kindness by pillorying her husband.

Anna's interests were not limited to the written word. She took lessons in painting; in 1669 Alexander Browne, her instructor, dedicated a treatise on painting to her, praising her 'grandeur' and 'sweetness of humor'. She became the patron of Sir Godfrey Kneller, who had been 'discovered' shortly after his arrival in England in 1676 by James Vernon, Monmouth's secretary. Kneller's style would certainly appeal far more than Lely's to a woman of Anna's temperament.

Until the children came Anna led a rather lonely life at Charles's dissolute court. She travelled with the king and his entourage when they left London for such fixtures as the autumn racing at Newmarket. She went on little outings, such as the visit to Deptford with Lord Admiral York in 1669, where, Pepys reported, York, his duchess, Anna, Castlemaine, and the other court ladies all sat around on the floor of the treasurer's house playing 'I love my love with an A'. The king was kind, and paid attention to her, perhaps to make up for his son's neglect. She accompanied Charles on his walks in the park. She was the hostess of the notorious supper party in Whitehall in June 1667 when, with the Dutch fleet threatening the fortifications of London, Charles and Lady Castlemaine, and presumably Anna too, were, said Pepys, 'all mad in hunting a poor moth' around the supper table. In September Charles bought Anna a coach that Lady Castlemaine no longer wanted, paying his mistress £145 for it. Anna reported the king's attentions to her mother, who wrote to Charles in December 1667 'to tell your Majesty how joyful it is to me that your Majesty doth so kindly notice my daughter'. Monmouth's increasingly public neglect and womanising sometimes drove her to the point of complaint to the king—for instance (if one believes one of the less reliable court gossips) on the occasion in the mid-1670s when Monmouth openly propositioned Moll Kirke, one of Mary of Modena's maids of honour, on an outing on a barge with Anna present. Moll Kirke was a highly accessible young woman who was sleeping with Anna's and Mary of Modena's husbands and the earl of Mulgrave; perhaps Anna complained because her husband had such bad taste. Moll's promiscuity caused trouble. Monmouth, learning that Mulgrave was his rival, had him arrested one night as he was returning home from Moll's embraces, and got Charles to replace him as commander of a regiment of guards. Mulgrave retaliated by informing York that he was sharing Moll with his nephew, which did not improve relations between them. Mulgrave was a nasty-minded troublemaker who insinuated in his memoirs that Anna became York's mistress in order to further Monmouth's career. He was the only person ever to suggest that Anna was unfaithful.

Anna throughout her long life never took very much interest in politics, and for a long time neither did Monmouth. His exceptional position led to appointments to the English privy council when he came of age in 1670, to the army council constituted in that year after Lord General Monck's death, and to the admiralty council of 1673, necessitated when the Test Act forced York's resignation as lord admiral. These were matters of routine, as was his appointment to the Scottish privy council in 1674. Less routine was his inclusion in a commission to negotiate with Sweden in 1674, his only diplomatic employment; apparently he was not much use to Arlington and the other professionals on the commission. His public career lay in the army, and it was his ambition to obtain the highest possible military command that began the permanent, and fatal, breach with his uncle the duke of York.

Monmouth's very existence, and the king's love for him, made York uneasy from the very beginning. As early as May 1663 Pepys reported a coolness between the royal brothers over him. Anna, as she grew to mature years, realised something that Monmouth never did: that Monmouth must not force the king into a situation where he had to choose between his son and his brother. York was the heir to the throne. Charles might heap indignities on his brother, send him to Scotland or into exile, but he would never deprive York of his place in the succession. Anna knew very well that it would be fatal to Monmouth, and to her and the children, if he made an irreconcilable enemy of York. She therefore strove with all her might to keep Monmouth out of politics. Besting York in the competition for Moll Kirke's readily granted favours was one thing; to ask Charles to grant him Monck's place as captain-general of the army was quite another. Monmouth first made the request in 1674, after his praiseworthy showing in the Dutch war. York did not like it. Charles's recent interest in the Roos divorce case (see above, pp. 75–76) had revived the stories about the little black box that allegedly contained Charles's and Lucy Walter's marriage lines.* 'These discourses,' wrote Burnet, 'were all carried to the duke of Monmouth, and got fatally into his head.' York professed not to worry. He told Burnet that he did not believe that Monmouth had the nerve to make a bid for the crown, and he had nothing but praise for Anna. 'Hopes of a crown could not work on her to do an unjust thing.'

Charles turned Monmouth's request aside in 1674, but in the spring of 1678, when Monmouth renewed his importunities, Charles granted it. The king was in desperate political trouble. French successes in the continental war, the king's ambivalent attitude to his new nephew-by-marriage, William of Orange, with whom he had recently signed a treaty, the suspicion—correct—that he was secretly dealing with Louis XIV, created an awful political situation. Monmouth was immensely popular, and a Protestant; the duke of York was neither. So Charles made his son captain-general and sent him to the continent with the forces that had been raised to succour William of Orange.

The duke of York was enraged. He had warned Monmouth that the appointment, if made, would cost Monmouth his friendship; he was still further angered to discover that in the wording of Monmouth's commission the word 'natural' before 'son' of the king had been scratched out. He complained to Charles, who destroyed the offending document but did not revoke the commission. Monmouth had won. He should have rested content with his victory. Instead, he made his first political move, the first step on the path to Tower Hill. He associated himself with the demand for the removal

---

* One of the oddest of these stories, recorded in a deposition taken by Leoline Jenkins in 1680, was that Henrietta Maria had consented to Charles's marriage to Lucy because he was literally dying of love for her and she would not give in without a wedding ring. Jenkins rightly regarded this as preposterous.

from office of Secretary Lauderdale, a man almost as unpopular in England as York, though for different reasons. Monmouth had joined the political opposition.

Anna tried desperately to prevent her husband from making a permanent enemy of his uncle. She tried to keep him away from the earl of Shaftesbury, the leader of the opposition, whose first effort to use Monmouth as a stalking-horse for his designs had come late in 1673, just after Charles dismissed him as lord chancellor. She cultivated York so assiduously that the gossips' tongues began to wag; Monmouth thereupon forbade her to see him. York was astonished and insulted; his disposition was not improved when the malicious Mulgrave told him that Monmouth's action was justified. Anna's efforts failed, and she took to spending more and more time at Moor Park. Her last child by Monmouth, born in 1678, was sickly; he was to die late in 1679. Not only were her efforts vain, they also appeared to be foolish, since Monmouth's new political career was apparently flourishing on account of his association with Shaftesbury. The dissolution of the Cavalier Parliament early in 1679 led to the great victory of Shaftesbury's party at the polls. In the spring of 1679 Charles sent Monmouth to Scotland to put down the rebellion that Lauderdale's policies had provoked there; Monmouth returned with great honour, an enhanced reputation, and a seat at Shaftesbury's side in a reconstituted privy council. York, meanwhile, was shipped over to Brussels in the vain hope that his physical removal from the scene would dampen the excitement, and the demand for his exclusion from the throne, which the Popish Plot had engendered. From Brussels York wrote gloomy letters to his son-in-law William of Orange. The king, he remarked in June 1679, was not at all pleased with Monmouth, 'but still continues kind in his mind to him', hoping that he would mend his behaviour.

Monmouth never did. The story of his disastrous political adventures has been told many times, and need not be retold here. What is often overlooked is the loyalty and forbearance of his wife. By the autumn of 1679 Monmouth had so irritated his father that Charles deprived him of the office of captain-general and ordered him into exile, at the same time sending York to Scotland, both to keep him out of England and to administer the kingdom in place of the ageing and unwell Lauderdale. Within two months Monmouth returned to England without permission and refused to obey the king's order to leave. Charles was understandably furious, and deprived him of all his profitable offices save that of master of the horse. Monmouth commented that he would have to live on Anna's money from now on, which indeed he did. He did spend some time with her at their Whitehall lodgings; their infant son was dying. Anna took advantage of their mutual sorrow to urge him to obey the king, but in vain. In the following year he began his affair with Lady Henrietta Wentworth and continued to defy his father—it was at this time that Nell Gwyn dubbed him Prince Perkin. Anna had had enough. Her health began to give way under the strain, though Charles's kindness cheered her—the king made it clear that he did not blame her for Monmouth's behaviour. Anna decided to do what others have done in similar circumstances: she travelled. On August 7, 1680, she received official permission to go to France with her three children (and thirty servants) to recover her health. By the end of the month she had arrived in Paris. Her illness was more than diplomatic. In January 1681 she wrote to Lord Melville asking him to stay on as her principal business agent in Scotland— he had managed the settlement with Tweeddale and the reduction of her dangerous marriage contract mentioned above (see above, pp. 94–95)—and concluding, 'I have been very ill of late. If I die, be kind to my children'.

Anna remained in France for two years, returning to her Whitehall lodgings in May 1682. She had some difficulties with French official-dom, which would not grant her a license to export her plate and held up some of the rest of her possessions at Calais: *plus ça change*. She got back to find her husband very angry with her because she had spent almost twice as much money in France as they had agreed she should: £11,261 instead of £6,000. The invaluable Sir Stephen Fox, according to his own account, persuaded the king to put up the whole amount. Anna also found Monmouth's political prospects much diminished. He was no longer master of the horse, Charles had just issued an order that no one was to deal with him, and he was forbidden to enter his Whitehall lodgings, although they were still open to Anna. The king also cut Monmouth's pension in half, from £8,000 to £4,000, and ordered the remaining half to be paid directly to Anna. Monmouth continued defiant. In September, dur-ing his 'progress' in Cheshire, he again touched for the king's evil, as he had on his western 'progress' in 1680. Charles ordered his ar-rest. He made bail, and actually spent a little time at Moor Park with his family. Once again Anna begged him to obey his father and end his dealings with Shaftesbury's associates—by this time the earl had fled to the United Provinces, where he died early in 1683. Once again Monmouth refused. The new year saw the beginning of the murky business known as the Rye House Plot. The extent of Monmouth's involvement is not clear; his biographers differ over whether he had agreed to, or was aware of, a plan to kill his father, if plan there was. When the plot broke, in June 1683, Monmouth was accused of involvement, and became a fugitive. He was formally accused of high treason, and a reward of £500 was offered for his arrest. He seems to have taken refuge briefly with his former mistress Eleanor Needham in Great Russell Street; then he holed up with Lady Henrietta and her mother at their house at Toddington, Bedfordshire, where he remained for several weeks.

The charge of high treason was a desperately serious matter for Anna: her children's future was at stake. Not only was her husband implicated in the plot, so also were her brothers-in-law, the indispensable Lord Melville and the earl of Tarras. Melville escaped arrest in Scotland, thanks to his and Anna's friend the future earl of Cromartie, and came to London to try to clear his name. The king was very cool to him, and this time he and one of his sons fell into the hands of the arresting officers. Anna's page, making extensive use of her name, pried them loose, and all three fled to the United Provinces, that common refuge of all the opponents of Charles's government. Melville was eventually denounced rebel and forfeited, but Anna persuaded the king to leave his movable property in the hands of his wife, who was Anna's half-sister. Tarras, as has been said, saved himself by a confession that sent another man to the scaffold (see above, p.55).

In July 1683, just after the revelation of the plot, there was a rumour that Monmouth had been seen at his Whitehall lodgings, where Anna was in residence. Burnet told the story that Charles came to see Anna and told her that the lodgings would be searched, but not her private rooms, so that Monmouth could hide there. Monmouth did not believe this, and left; the private rooms were indeed searched. When Burnet's history was published, Anna declared the story untrue; it turned out that Burnet had heard it from a man who had got it from Monmouth himself. Anna was surely telling the truth, because the fact is that Charles did not want Monmouth arrested, and had no interest in trapping him. All the world knew where Monmouth was hiding. Charles ordered Lord Bruce, the future earl of Ailesbury, whose family lived near Toddington, to go there and arrest Monmouth. Bruce demurred: the place was a maze, with far too many means of escape. So Charles cancelled the order.

The king still loved his son; what he wanted was confession and submission. Once again, and for the last time, Anna strove to save her foolish husband from himself and his delusive ambitions, which, comments Antonia Fraser, 'in view of Monmouth's behavior as a husband . . . was indeed gracious behavior on her part'. She very nearly succeeded. Monmouth wrote the king a penitent letter, delivered by the earl of Halifax, who also was working for a reconciliation. He then addressed a second letter, quite possibly written by Halifax, to Charles, sent it to Anna, and asked her to deliver it. On October 15, 1683, she sent it to the king 'since I am so unhappy as to have no hopes of seeing your Majesty', pleading for her errant husband. So did Queen Catherine. Halifax continued to play the go-between. At last, on November 25, father and son met. Monmouth signed the necessary confession and asked forgiveness of his father and his uncle. Charles immediately pardoned him and gave him a present of £6,000. For a day or two a happy ending was in sight; Monmouth and Anna took up residence in Whitehall again. Then, at York's insistence, Monmouth's confession, which implicated others, was published in the official *Gazette*. Monmouth lost his head and publicly repudiated his confession. Charles angrily insisted that he reconfirm it in writing. Halifax and Anna went to work again; Monmouth signed the necessary paper, had second thoughts, and demanded that the king return it to him. Charles at last lost his temper, called his son a blockhead, and ordered him from the court. On December 7, 1683, Anna and Monmouth left Whitehall, he for the last time until he returned, his uncle's prisoner, to grovel for his life. They went to Moor Park. Within a month Monmouth was once again a refugee from his father's kingdoms. Lady Henrietta followed him abroad. Anna never saw him again until their final interviews in the Tower.

Anna was in a very unhappy position, the wife of a fugitive who was almost, but not quite, a condemned traitor. She did not suffer materially. Charles had made it clear to the Scottish privy council that his prohibition against dealing with Monmouth did not apply to her, and that she was to continue to receive the income from her estates. Between December 1683 and August 1684 Anna received £5,000 from the excise, the money Monmouth used to receive, although Charles never cut him off completely. Monmouth's attempt to sell the reversion rights in a Lincolnshire estate that he and Anna were to receive on Queen Catherine's death was blocked, and in January 1685 Charles set up a trust, with Sir Stephen Fox as its manager, comprising these lands and other land granted to Monmouth in 1673 to round out the Hedge Lane property in London. Anna publicly dissociated herself from her husband. On Christmas Day, 1683, by which time Monmouth may have left England, she took communion at St. James's with Princess Anne and others, including John Evelyn, who noted the fact in his diary.* In May 1684 Queen Catherine received her very kindly. At the end of the year, perhaps because she had picked up reports of Monmouth's quick, clandestine trip to England, when he saw his father for the last time, she wrote to Charles, asking about the possibility of Monmouth's recall. Charles replied that the time was not ripe. Many people, including William of Orange, thought that it soon would be. Monmouth was 'the Delilah of this place', wrote the secretary of the English ambassador at The Hague on January 28, 1685, 'and is daily more and more caressed by the prince' and others too. But when Charles died nine days later, Anna and William and everybody else knew that Monmouth had no future in his uncle's three kingdoms. William told him that he would have to leave the United Provinces, and advised him to take service in the armies of the Emperor Leopold, now fighting against the Turks. Instead Prince Perkin took the road to Sedgemoor.

The new king and queen were Anna's friends. In March 1685 she formally introduced her eldest son to them, and when she went to Mary of Modena to 'deplore the sadness of her condition', James assured her that Sir Stephen Fox would continue to look after her. She was in residence in Whitehall with the children in June, when Monmouth landed in western England and proclaimed himself king. James at once made sure of the children: guards were posted at the Whitehall lodgings on June 16, and early in July he ordered their transfer to the Tower. Anna accompanied them. There she had ample time to think, to reflect upon her twenty-two years of marriage to a spoiled child

---

* Princess Mary, when she left England as the wife of William of Orange, asked Anna to take care of her younger sister, now the only Protestant in the royal family. Anna frequently attended St. James's chapel. She was not pious, but her Protestantism was never in doubt.

who inspired so much love in so many of those around him. Did Anna, too, love him, in spite of everything? He had given her every reason in the world not to, and there is no doubt that he did not love her, had never loved her. At the end he rather meanly argued that she did not love him because, during his years of adversity, she had been seen in public, at the theatre and elsewhere. He was nearer to the truth when he observed that Anna 'was imposed upon him when he was very young and not by his own choice and that she was his wife by law but the other [Lady Henrietta] was his wife before God'. They had indeed been married too young to know their own minds. Did Anna come to know, in her own mind, that she loved Monmouth? During his life she never gave any indication, by word or deed, that she did not, though his conduct mightily offended her, and she showed it. She was faithful and loyal. And afterwards she was silent. 'I will not speak of what is past forever', she would say when asked about the duke. So we shall never know. *Le coeur a ses raisons* . . .

EPILOGUE: THE WIDOWED DUCHESS

Anna lived for over forty years after she buried Prince Perkin. In many ways it was a very different sort of life. She was no longer royalty. She had to vacate the apartments in Whitehall, which went to James's naval commander, Lord Dartmouth. Her immediate preoccupation was the restoration of the Buccleuch estate. The earl of Moray, the Scottish secretary of state, predicted within two weeks of Monmouth's execution that 'there will be favor enough shown to the widow and children', and he was right. King James, after a momentary pause—he inquired whether a Scottish estate could be forfeited in consequence of a condemnation in England—allowed justice and friendship to prevail. He authorised Anna's acquisition of whatever plate and jewels Monmouth had left behind in Holland, and in May 1686 he instructed the Scottish privy council to stop inquiring into what part of the Buccleuch estate fell to him by forfeiture, in view of Anna's 'exemplary loyalty, unblameable deportment, and constant duty'. Thus Anna was able to keep such property as the barony of Hawick, which was confiscable because it had been acquired after the regrant of 1666 which vested the estate in her in her own right. She kept her annual pension of £4,000.* She would have liked to have had the Monmouth title restored as well, and after the revolution of 1688 she asked King William to do this. Not surprisingly, William refused: the inference might be drawn that the late duke was no traitor, and so, perhaps, legitimate. To forestall further discussion he gave the title of earl of Monmouth to Lord Mordaunt on the ground of his descent from Robert Carey, created earl of Monmouth by James I.

Anna was a young woman in 1685, only thirty-four, and it is not surprising that she thought of marrying again. In May 1688, three months after her mother's death, she did. Her choice was a man she knew well, Charles, Lord Cornwallis, four years her junior, the widower of the daughter of Sir Stephen Fox. One of the poetical

* All the monetary figures in the epilogue are in pounds sterling.

wits* predictably seized on this to have some fun at Anna's expense—since she was no longer royalty she was fair game:

> Justly, false Monmouth, did thy Lord declare
> Thou shouldst not in his crown nor empire share;
> Indeed, dear Limp, it was a just design,
> Seeing he had so small a share of thine.

After running through a catalogue of her supposed lovers he concludes:

> Cornwallis next succeeds the lovely train,
> And round his neck displays a captive's chain.
> He, greater fool than any of the rest,
> They say, will marry with the trimming beast.
> Which, if he does, oh, may his blood be shed
> On that high throne where her last traitor bled!

The marriage lasted ten years, until Cornwallis's death in 1688 at the comparatively early age of forty-three. There were three children, two of whom died young; thus Anna, like her mother, gave birth to many children (nine), of whom few (three) survived to adulthood. There were money troubles in plenty. Anna was still extravagant and still in debt, thanks in part to the fact that, as he said he would, Monmouth had indeed lived on her money after the stream of royal largesse dried up. Her affairs had become rather chaotic of late. Her stepfather Earl David, a competent businessman, had died in 1679 and her estate manager, Lord Melville, was in exile until 1688 in consequence of the Rye House Plot. Her new husband had misspent his youth drinking and gambling, and at one point was actually tried as accessory to a murder. He was acquitted; evidently the shock of being on trial for his life, and his marriage to Fox's daughter, sobered him, and he behaved more moderately thereafter. But his marriage to Anna set off a new wave of spending; in a year they found themselves £30,000 in debt. Fox, for the sake of his grandchildren, took their affairs in hand. It was an uphill struggle. Matters came to a head in 1694, when there was so little cash, and Anna's credit was so bad, that she had difficulty paying for her son's wedding. Fox wrote that 'so many wants and necessities appeared' as to be embarrassing. There was a tearful scene;

---

* The editor of *Poems on Affairs of State*, vol. IV (1685–1688), Galbraith Crump, attributes the poem to Charles Sackville, earl of Dorset.

Fox, with Lord Melville's cooperation, at last persuaded her that she would have to economise.

When Cornwallis died four years later, all her accumulated resentment at the self-made upstart who had been dictating her financial behaviour burst out. Fox, as part of the arrangements for the funeral, which he paid for, set up a coat of arms which crossed that of Cornwallis with those of his daughter and Anna. Anna was furious, had it pulled down, and the offending escutcheon of Fox's daughter removed, to the accompaniment of violent and pejorative language about her and her son, the new Lord Cornwallis. Anna was, wrote Fox, wholly governed by 'rage, passion, and self-interest'. Especially, he thought, self-interest: she added injury to insult by ordering that Fox should not receive another penny from her estates, even though she owed him £1,500. Fox was convinced that her rage was simulated: she had provoked the quarrel purely in order to bilk him. This is unlikely, since at one point she offered the shame-faced excuse that in removing Fox's daughter's escutcheon she was following the requirements of Earl Francis's entail. Fox promptly exploded this by getting an opinion from Scotland to the effect that her behaviour 'would have been looked on as a riot, and the injustice punished with great severity'. Whatever Anna's motives, her treatment of a man who had been involved in her affairs for over thirty years and had repeatedly bailed her out of financial difficulty was both mean and shabby.*

Anna was once again a widow. Her connection with the court had become rather tenuous after the death of her friend Queen Mary, whom she praised as having 'all good qualities man or woman could have'. It became more tenuous still after the death of Cornwallis, a steadfast Whig who stood well with King William. So in 1701 she decided to go to Scotland, for the first time since she had journeyed south as the prospective bride of the king's bastard in 1662. She always talked sentimentally about Scotland, and boasted of her 'Scotch heart'. Now, Scotland had something to offer that England did not: a pre-eminent social position. In Scotland she could behave

---

* Fox further alleged, in one of his many versions of this episode, that Anna laid hands on her late husband's jewels and plate and the arrears of his pension, so that the new Lord Cornwallis was left with nothing movable but the sheep and cattle on his estate, 'and hath neither spoon nor napkin'. Fox did not give up trying to get his money; he and Anna were still arguing about who owed whom, and how much, in 1710.

as a royal personage, which she could no longer do in England. There was also the matter of becoming personally acquainted with her kinfolk and tenants. She was the head of the family; her long absence in England and her neglect of the chief's obligation to help needy dependents drew disapproving comment from the family poet, Scott of Satchells. So she settled in at Dalkeith and set about rebuilding it on a lavish scale. 'You will think me extravagant in marble,' she wrote Melville, 'but it is to show you I do not despise my old Castle.' It was indeed redone in marble, including the adorning of her bedroom with carvings by Grinling Gibbons. Anna's architect was James Smith, who by coincidence was simultaneously rebuilding Yester House for the son of Anna's old enemy Tweeddale, now dead. The rebuilding of Dalkeith took the better part of a decade. In the process it ceased to be called a castle and became a 'palace', a label still used in the guidebooks: Anna was royalty. She styled herself 'Mighty Princess' in some of her charters to the town. Her cousin Margaret Montgomery, dining with her, remarked that Anna was served on bended knee. She, as Anna's relative, was allowed to sit; everyone else stood.

As she grew older Anna became increasingly suspicious of what she believed to be attempts to deprive her of what was rightfully hers. In the 1690s she sued the heirs of her stepfather and her uncle Rothes for what she alleged was the looting of her estate (see above, pp.51, 68). In 1704 she quarrelled bitterly with Lord Melville. He was her sister's husband; he had been immensely useful to her for over twenty years; he had suffered severe personal injury, to his right hand and arm, in 1700 when he saved her charter chest from destruction by fire. No matter: Anna convinced herself that Melville had mishandled her money, would not listen to explanations, and began a lawsuit that was not settled until 1711, four years after Melville's death. She resolutely refused to follow the example of that other Scottish duchess, Anne of Hamilton, who had asked King Charles to create her husband duke of Hamilton and, four years after his death, transferred the title to her eldest son. Neither Cornwallis nor Anna's son and heir (who predeceased her) ever became duke of Buccleuch. Anna dismissed such suggestions out of hand. 'Till I change my mind,' she wrote Melville in 1698 when, with Cornwallis dead, it was suggested that she emulate the duchess of Hamilton, 'I will keep all the rights I enjoy from God and my forefathers . . . The Duchess of Hamilton is but a woman, and we are not such wise creatures as men, so I will follow no example of that sort till I see all the noblemen in Scotland resign to their sons, then I will consider of the business.' Two months later she reiterated her position even more firmly. 'I . . . will never be so blinded whilst I keep my reason as to lesson myself in my own family, but will keep my authority and be the head of it whilst it please God to give me life . . . . I am sure you laugh at your sister, for so I am to you, but a man in my own family.' She remained duchess of Buccleuch to the end.

The end was long in coming. Anna outlived her eldest son, her daughter-in-law, even her grandson's wife, who, sadly, died of small-pox in 1729. 'She was as good a young woman as ever I knew in all my life,' wrote Anna. For all of her 'Scotch heart'—she disapproved of what she called 'this unlucky Union' of 1707—Anna preferred London. After the change of dynasty in 1714 she found reason to re-main there. She quickly became very friendly with the new Princess of Wales, Caroline of Ansbach, that very clever lady who, like Anna, was married to a king's son notorious, like his father, for his infidelities. 'The Princess loved her mightily,' wrote Lady Cowper in her diary in 1716, 'and certainly no woman of her years deserved it so well. She had all the life and fire of youth, and it was marvellous to see that the many afflictions she had suffered had not touched her wit and good nature, but at upwards of three score she had both in their full perfection.' Her finances recovered, and she added to the family property, most notably the lordship of Melrose, which she purchased from the earl of Haddington. She was one of the last survivors of the court of Charles II, and she dined out on stories about the king and the virago Castlemaine and pretty, witty Nell—though never Prince Perkin—till her death in London in February 1732, just before her eighty-first birthday. As with her grandfather Earl Walter almost exactly a century before, her body was trans-ported from London to Scotland, where it lies in the family vault in St. Nicholas' Church on the High Street of Dalkeith. There is no mention of Monmouth on the plate on her coffin.

AFTERWORD: CLOSING THE FAMILY ALBUM

The tale of the Buccleuch heiresses is one episode in the long history of an aristocratic family. The history continues: there is still a duke of Buccleuch, and he is still the owner of many thousands of acres and the 'palace' of Dalkeith, though it is no longer his principal residence. Our story has encompassed two generations and many people who were related to Mary and Anna: their husbands, Tarras and Monmouth, their husbands' fathers, Haychesters and King Charles, their father and mother, their stepfather Lord Wemyss, their uncle Rothes, their aunt Lady Tweeddale and her husband, the Tweeddales' son, their first cousin and disappointed suitor, who married Lauderdale's daughter, their half-brother by marriage Lord Melville, Anna's uncle by marriage the duke of York. Virtually every major player in the drama of the two little girls left so early fatherless and rich was kin to them in one way or another.

This circumstance prompts reflection on the place of family history in Clio's larger scheme. Lawrence Stone regards it as central to an understanding of the historical process, and his remarkable and diverse output over the past thirty years has gone far to demonstrate the truth of his opinion. What Mary's and Anna's story illustrates is the crucial connection between family and politics, at least as far as this family is concerned. At every stage in the story of these two children the political situation was decisive in determining their destiny. The swingeing fine that the Protectorate levied on the Buccleuch estate on account of Earl Francis's political behaviour afforded Tweeddale his opportunity to involve himself in the family's affairs. The death of Oliver Cromwell prompted Lady Wemyss, who feared Tweeddale's influence with the new Lord Protector, to arrange Mary's illegal marriage. The restoration of the monarchy enabled Rothes to cut himself in through the gambit of wardship. It also enabled Lady Wemyss to foil the hated Tweeddale once more, because the new king had a bastard son for Anna to marry. The successful ratification of their marriage contract in parliament helped make Lauderdale's political career. When Tweeddale's political star rose, thanks in part to a helpful marriage for his son with Lauderdale's daughter, he was able to drive a satisfactory financial bargain over his debt to the Buccleuchs. When he lost his political influence, in part because of a quarrel with his new in-laws over a legacy, the financial bargain was torn up and he was ultimately forced to pay. Anna's husband's political folly opened the door one last time for her uncle Tweeddale, only to have her other uncle King James firmly close it.

What all this suggests is that historians of the family—at least of the aristocratic family—must pay close attention to politics. And by the same token political historians must remember that every player on the political stage is a member of a family, and that his or her attitude toward the members of that family can be enormously important. Antonia Fraser has demonstrated that Mary Queen of Scots was taught to rely on her relatives; she found, to her sorrow, that her Scottish kin were not as supportive as her French ones, for good political reasons in both cases. Even Mary's kinswoman and rival, the Virgin Queen, was not immune to family considerations. Suppose Elizabeth had liked her cousins Mary and Catherine Grey instead of detesting them: what might have happened to the English succession? Elizabeth was wise to understand that family considerations and family ambition ate into, not so much men's loyalty to her, as their single-mindedness in her service: it was not merely old maid's jealousy that caused her to fly into a rage if someone around her married. If political considerations drove family decisions, as with Lady Wemyss, family considerations and arrangements motivated politicians like Lauderdale, and created political networks like that put together by Lauderdale's grandfather Lord Chancellor Dunfermline. Political office could make a family aristocratic, as it had the Maitlands, and, in England, the Cecils and the Hydes, among others. The risen family then scrambles to cement its political and social position by making aristocratic marriages. The right marriage can rescue a political career—so thought Sir Edward Coke when he compelled his daughter to marry the half-witted brother of King James I's current favourite. And of course the great political crisis of the reign of Charles II turned on one simple familial fact: the barrenness of Catherine of Braganza.

The welfare of a family depends upon the marriages it makes: an obvious point upon which every historian of the family, and of women, has dwelt. These historians normally, and rightly, stress economic and social considerations; the politics of such alliances, save where royal weddings are concerned, is sometimes overlooked. For example, there is a study waiting to be done on the marital politics of King James VI and I: not only marriages between English and Scots, to which Keith Brown has given some attention in an article in the 1993 *Historical Journal,* but also those between English families—and Scottish families too. These marriages were not made in heaven; their loci were the family council chamber and the lawyer's office. That so many of them worked reasonably well is testimony to the resilience of human beings; that others, like Anna's, failed should be no cause for surprise.

If there is a generalisation to be drawn from the life stories of Mary and Anna Scott, it is that in a dynastic age family, marriage, and politics are inseparable. This is no startling or revolutionary conclusion. But then, what I promised was a good story, nothing more. If you, the reader, have found that in these pages, and perhaps a little food for thought as well, I am content.

APPENDIX A: NOTE ON THE SOURCES

Pride of place must go to Sir William Fraser, *The Scotts of Buccleuch*, 2 vols. (1878). Like all twenty-four of his histories of Scottish aristocratic families, it contains biographical sketches of the heads of the family and prints many documents. The account of Mary's life is more useful than that of Anna's, because Fraser made extensive use of the papers of the Scotts of Harden, the branch of the family that included Mary's husband Tarras and his father Haychesters. These papers are now in the Scottish Record Office (henceforth SRO), GD 157. Fraser had access also to the Wemyss papers (*Memorials of the Family of Wemyss of Wemyss*, 3 vols., 1888), which are now, unfortunately, unavailable for research. Two of Fraser's other works were also helpful: *The Melvilles Earls of Melville and the Leslies Earls of Leven*, 3 vols. (1890), and *The Earls of Cromartie*, 2 vols. (1876).

Fraser's principal source for the Scott family was the Buccleuch archive, much of which is in SRO, GD 224. The Historical Manuscripts Commission has printed five volumes of Buccleuch manuscripts, mostly seventeenth-century material, but there is not much in them relevant for this book. Fraser did not make use of the two manuscript sources most useful to me. One is the very large collection of Lauderdale papers in the British Library, Add. Mss. 23113–23138, 23242–23251, 35125. The printed collection of Lauderdale papers, which Osmund Airy edited for the Camden Society, 3 vols. (1884–85), is of no help, since Airy concentrated exclusively on politics and religion. The second collection is the even larger repository of Tweeddale manuscripts in the National Library of Scotland. It would be futile to list all the manuscripts in this collection from which I drew material. A few that are particularly important are Mss. 7023, Lauderdale's letters to Tweeddale, 7024–30, Tweeddale's letterbooks, 7109, his autobiography, 14542–45, his relations with the Buccleuchs, and 14546–50, his relations with Lauderdale, for which 3134 and 3177 are important also. There is a useful collection of Yester writs in SRO, GD 28. There are other significant manuscripts in both the British Library (notably Add. Mss. 51326 and 51327, Fox's accounts of his dealings with Anna) and the National

Library of Scotland (notably Mss. 597, a miscellany of Lauderdale papers).

Among the important printed sources are the *Register of the Privy Council of Scotland*, 3rd series, 13 vols., 1661–1689, ed. P. Hume Brown *et al* (1908–32), *The Acts of the Parliaments of Scotland*, vols. VII, VIII, ed. T. Thomson (1820), *Calendar of State Papers, Domestic*, 31 vols., 1660–1689, ed. M. A. E. Green *et al* (1860–1972), and *Calendar of Treasury Books*, 8 vols., some in many parts, ed. W. A. Shaw (1904–23), covering the reigns of Charles II and James II. Various reports of the Historical Manuscripts Commission were used through consultation of its indices. Other useful collections of letters and papers include *The Calendar of the Clarendon State Papers*, 5 vols., ed. H. O. Coxe and C. Firth (1869–70), two compilations of Lauderdale correspondence not in the British Library made by Henry Paton, printed in the *Miscellany of the Scottish History Society* V (1933) and VI (1939), and Robert Baillie, *Letters and Journals*, 3 vols., ed. D. Laing, Bannatyne Club (1841–42).

The important diaries and memoirs are *The Diary of John Lamont of Newton 1649–71*, ed. G. R. Kinloch, Maitland Club (1830), John Nichol, *A Diary of Public Transactions*, ed. D. Laing, Bannatyne Club (1836), Sir George Mackenzie, *Memoirs of the Affairs of Scotland*, ed. T. Thomson (1821), Samuel Pepys, *Diary*, 11 vols., ed. R. Latham and W. Matthews (1970–83), John Evelyn, *Diary*, 6 vols., ed. E. S. de Beer (1955), Mary, Countess Cowper, *Diary*, ed. Spenser Cowper, 2nd ed. (1865), *Memoirs of Thomas, Earl of Ailesbury, written by Himself*, 2 vols., ed. W. E. Buckley, Roxburghe Club (1890), *The Life of James the Second*, 2 vols., ed. J. S. Clarke (1816), *The Works of John Sheffield, Earl of Mulgrave, Marquis of Normanby, and Duke of Buckingham*, 2 vols. (1723), Henry Sidney, *The Diary of the Times of Charles the Second*, 2 vols., ed. R. W. Blencowe (1893), and James Wellwood, *Memoirs* (1700). The contemporary account of Anna's final interviews with Monmouth in the Tower is in George Rose, *Observations on the Historical Work of the late Rt. Hon. Charles James Fox* (1809).

The most important poetical compilation is *Poems on Affairs of State*, 4 vols., covering 1660–1688, ed. G. de F. Lord *et al* (1963–68). There are also Walter Scott of Satchells, *A True History of several honourable families of the name of Scot (sic)*, ed. J. G. Winning (1894), and John Wilmot, earl of Rochester, *Poems on Several Occasions*, ed. J. Thorpe (1950), his dirty poetry, conveniently collected in one volume. Buckingham's satire on the king quoted in Chapter 7 may be found in J. H. Wilson, *The Court Wits of the Restoration* (1948), a delightful and informative book.

Two important contemporary historians must be mentioned: the earl of Clarendon, *The History of the Rebellion and Civil Wars in England*, 6 vols., ed. W. D. Macray (1888) and *The Life of Edward, earl of Clarendon . . . Written by Himself*, 2 vols. (1760), and Gilbert Burnet, *The History of My Own Time*, 2 vols., ed. O. Airy (1897–1900).

I have consulted a very large number of secondary works in the preparation of this book; it is impossible to mention them all. Three indispensable reference works are the *Dictionary of National Biography*, J. Balfour Paul, *The Scots Peerage*, 9 vols. (1904–14), and G. E. C (ockayne), *The Complete Peerage*, new edn., ed. V. Gibbs *et al* (1910–59). The background for Mary's and Anna's story is best found in David Stevenson, *The Scottish Revolution 1637–44* (1973) and *Revolution and Counter-revolution in Scotland 1644–51* (1977), F. D. Dow, *Cromwellian Scotland 1651–1660* (1979), and D. Ogg, *England in the Reign of Charles II*, 2nd edn., 2 vols. (1959–60). There is no thorough study of politics in Restoration Scotland, though there is useful material in R. Hutton, *Charles II, King of England, Scotland, and Ireland* (1989) and in W. C. Mackenzie, *The Life and Times of John Maitland, Duke of Lauderdale* (1923). This book is in many ways out of date; Lauderdale badly needs a new biography. A work that should be in print is Roy Lennox, 'Lauderdale and Scotland: A Study in Restoration Politics and Administration 1660–1682,' Ph.D. dissertation, Columbia University (1977). A useful work for the last decade of the century is P. W. J. Riley, *King William and the Scottish Politicians* (1979). No Scottish political figure save Lauderdale has attracted a biographer, and there are not all that many useful ones, for the purposes of this book, among those of Englishmen. Among the helpful ones are John Miller, *Charles II* (1991) and Antonia Fraser, *King Charles II* (1979) in addition to Hutton's study already mentioned. Miller has also written about the court in *Bourbon and Stuart* (1987), and has a biography of *James II: A Study in Kingship* (1978). The best biography of Monmouth is Elizabeth D'Oyley, *James Duke of Monmouth* (1938); I also found that of Bryan Bevan with the same title (1973) helpful. Also useful were C. H. Hartmann, *Charles II and Madame* (1934), Julia Cartwright, *Madame* (1901), James Winn, *John Dryden and His World* (1987), J. H. Wilson (on Buckingham), *A Rake and His Times* (1954), Doreen Cripps (on the duchess of Lauderdale), *Elizabeth of the Sealed Knot* (1975), Graham Greene, *Lord Rochester's Monkey*

(1974, though written earlier), and Christopher Clay, *Private Finance and Public Wealth: The Career of Sir Stephen Fox 1627–1716* (1978). Finally, for the position of women in the seventeenth century the essential works are Lawrence Stone, *The Family, Sex, and Marriage in England 1500–1800* (1977), Rosalind Marshall, *Virgins and Viragos, A History of Women in Scotland from 1080 to 1980* (1983), and Antonia Fraser, *The Weaker Vessel: Women's Lot in Seventeenth-Century England* (1985).

APPENDIX B: 'UGLY MEG, OR THE ROBBER'S WEDDING'

This is the poem written by Lady Louisa Stuart (see p. 6n.). It is printed in Fraser's *Scotts of Buccleuch*, vol. I, pp. lxxiii–lxxiv.

Peace to these worthy days of old,
Cast in our modern teeth so oft,
When Man was, as befits him, bold,
And Woman, as she should be, soft.

Those virtuous, upright, simple days,
When lucre—despicable thing—
Made never youth his finger raise,
Or fair, put hers in wedding ring.

Then worth was all that Parents weighed,
And Damsels listened not to lies;
And suitors wished a lovely maid
To bring no dowry but her eyes.

Then blessed was marriage, could it choose
When genuine Love, not crabbed Law,
Towering above all sordid views,
The contract came alone to draw,

Without one syllable of these,
Devised by Satan for our sins—
Entail and jointure and trustees,
And separate purses for—for pins.

Then wives accepted as a boon
What husbands' bounty loved to shower,
And widows broke their hearts too soon
To need the comforts of a dower.

Well! thus while stage and press declaim,
By pulpit on a Sunday backed,
Suppose we start some other game,
And rummage record-chests for fact.

What says the bard, whose witching song
Comes glowing with such vivid fires
As make the coldest of us long
To *warraie* [make war] like our gallant sires?

'Tis thus he says—but says in prose,
While only gladd'ning social hours—
The Cumbrian bugle loudly blows,
The chief returns with all his powers.

That blast bespeaks not rout or fear,
'Tis triumph's animating tone;
It scarcely meets the lady's ear,
When up she's to the rampart flown.

By this her lord has reach'd the moat,
Shouts for the bridge and quits his steed.
'What luck?' she asks; 'by all I note
Saint George was with you at your need.'

'None better, dame, might man desire;
We've chased the Borderers past their bounds,
Ta'en for us herds and goodly hire—
Rich payment for our ravaged grounds.

''Tis true the blue-caps showed us sport,
And breathful many a brave man's veins;
But see yon gallant, mark his port,
'Tis Scott of Harden in our chains.'

'Then be the Virgin praised,' she said,
'This day shall chronicler record.
Now, hark ye, ere the feast we spread,
What will you do with Harden's Lord?'

'Do!' cries the Baron, fierce,
'Do with a cut-throat and a thief?
The country's dread, the Border's curse,
Do with him? Let his prayers be brief.

'Here chuse me some convenient tree,
And hang him high ere break of day.'
'Nay, that they shall not do,' quoth she,
'Hang Harden's Knight—hang you they may.'

Oh, sweetness of the gentle sex
Melting with pity, lenient still,
And loveliest when its pleading checks
Bloodthirsty man's inhuman will.

'So!' the mild fair resumed, and placed
Her arms akimbo as she spake,
'Here's thrifty doings—war and waste
And brew the more the less you bake.

'Hang Harden's chief! a precious jest,
A bachelor comely, young, and rich;
You! with three maiden daughters blest,
Ill favoured as the nightmare each.

'Unbind his hands and fetch a friar—
I sleep not till the thing be done;
He takes his choice, and I acquire
The knight of Harden for my son.'

'Mass! though a woman, thou hast wit,'
The Baron said, and weighed the case,
'Yet sweetheart, an I must submit,
No chusing—that were too much grace.

'For Moll and Maudlin they may win
Some Christian husband, bad or good;
But ugly Meg would frighten sin,
And Harden weds her by the Rood.

'Black Ralph, thou hast a penman's fame,
Write articles on yonder drum,
When see thou bar the bridegroom's claim
To all I have, or have to come.

'No portion—but if Meg survives
He jointures her in all his lands;
So now pluck off the prisoner's gyves,
And, Father Topas, join their hands.'

'Stay, leave me thus forever bound,'
The captive in a panic cried,
'Or make me turn a mill-wheel round,
Ere yon Hobgoblin be my bride.'

'Hold!' quoth the Father, 'choice is just,
Prefer the gallows and do well,
A rope on Harden will, I trust,
Keep Meg from leading apes in hell.'

The priests now sung the parting hymn,
The noose was slipp'd beneath his head,
Ah! fair is life, though Meg be grim,
'Stop, stop,' he roars, 'I'll wink and wed.'

Thus wooed they in the good old days;
And, pitying reader, though you stare,
The last, the sweetest minstrel says,
These lived and died a loving pair.

GLOSSARY

Annualrent: interest income.

Cess: a monthly assessment levied on the Scots during the English occupation.

Clause irritant: the clause in Earl Francis's entail which extruded a future female holder of the estate who attempted to alter the entail.

Court of session: the highest Scottish civil court.

Cum maritagio **land**: land held of a superior which carries with it the right of wardship if the heir is a minor or female.

Curators: in Scots law those appointed by a minor heir or heiress on reaching the age of 12 to look after the estate until s/he turns 21.

Engagement: the agreement of December 1647 by which the Scots undertook to restore Charles I to his three thrones in return for his promise to establish presbyterianism in England for thre years and various commercial concessions.

Executry: the movables and personal property of the deceased which fall to the deceased's executor(s).

Jointure: land (usually) that a groom's family bestows upon newly-weds.

Liferent: income for life, usually from land.

Merk: two-thirds of a pound, or 13 shillings 4 pence.

Salvo jure cuiuslibet: an act routinely passed by the Scottish parliament at the end of each session protecting the legal rights of anyone who might be harmed by a private act passed during the session.

Tailzie: an entail.

Tocher: dowry.

Tutors: in Scots law the guardians of a minor heir or heiress, normally named in the deceased's will.

INDEX

Act of Pardon and Grace, 17, 23, 26
Act of Supremacy, 92
admiralty council, 111
Ailesbury, earl of, 97, 115
Albemarle, duke of, 104
Alexander, Lady, 35
Andrews, Lancelot, 107
Anna, duchess of Buccleuch, *see*
  Scott, Anna,
Anne of Denmark, 73
Argyll, marquis of, 12, 15, 35, 41,
  45, 49, 80
Arlington, Secretary of State, 62,
  96, 98, 111
Armstrong, Kinmont Willie, 5
army council, 111
Audley End, 106

Backwell, Alderman, 100
Baillie, Robert, 37
Balgonie, Lord, 31, 32, 57
Bath, 88, 90, 105
Bennet, Sir Henry, 87, 88, 89, 90
Berkeley, Charles, earl of
  Falmouth, 101
Berwick, duke of, 101
Blagge, Margaret, 108
Blair, Robert, 39
Borthwick, Dr., 36
Bothwell estate, 5, 8
Branxholm estate, 8
Bristol, 105
Browne, Alexander, 110
Bruce, Lord, 115
Brussels, 104, 113
Buccleuch estates, 3, 5, 6, 8–10
  (entail of), 13, 16, 24, 26, 29, 33,

34, 38, 42–44, 46, 50, 53, 56, 57,
  64, 66, 68, 71, 79, 86, 94–96, 100,
  104, 116, 119–122
Buckingham, duke of, 102, 103,
  107
Burnet, Bishop Gilbert, 19, 92, 93,
  112, 115

Calisto, play, 109
Callander, earl of, 17
Cambridge University, 101
Campbell, Neil, 35
captain-general of the army, 112,
  113
Carey, Robert, earl of Monmouth,
  119
Caroline of Ansbach, Princess of
  Wales, 123
Carteret, Sir George, 75
Cassillis, countess of, 35
Castlemaine, Lady, 65, 66, 70, 103,
  108–110, 123
Catherine of Braganza, Queen, 65,
  85, 99, 106, 108, 116, 117
cess, the, 16
Charing Cross, 72
Charles I, King, 7, 8, 11, 12, 20,
  21, 37, 62, 80
Charles II, King, 2, 12, 16, 21, 43–
  46, 49, 50, 53–55, 57–66, 68–73,
  75, 79–93, 95, 99, 99–107, 109–118
Cheshire, 114
Chiffinch, Will, 101
child mortality, 120
Chiswick, 100
Clarendon, earl of, 80, 81, 87–90
Clergy, Scottish, 39

Cleveland, Duchess of, 54
commissary court, 34, 37–39, 42
commissioners for the
    administration of justice, 34–5,
    38, 39
committee of estates, 17
Commons, the, 107
Corneille, 109
Cornwallis, Charles, Lord, 98,
    109, 119–121
Cornwallis, Lord, his son, 121,
    122
council, Scottish, 81
court of Charles II, 75, 79, 84, 88,
    96, 99–103, 106, 108–110, 116,
    123
court of James I, 107
court of session, 49, 52, 53, 64, 83,
    90, 95
Covenanters, 8, 9, 11, 20, 45, 57,
    63, 80
Covent Garden, 65
Coventry, Sir John, 103, 107
Cowper, Lady, 123
Crawford, earl of, 9, 56, 81, 82
Cromartie, earl of, 95, 97, 115
Cromwell, Oliver, 12, 13, 18, 23,
    24, 26–28, 30, 49, 62
Cromwell, Richard, 30, 37, 38, 40,
    41, 47
curators to Anna, 70, 71, 72, 85
curators to Monmouth, 100

Dalkeith, countess of, 95
Dalkeith, lordship of, 8, 12, 14,
    24, 32, 35–37, 58, 122
Dalkeith Palace, 122, 124
dancing, 104–5
Darnley, Lord, 15
Dartmouth, Lord, 119
debt, Tweeddale, 21, 26, 27, 42,
    51, 57, 94, 95
Deptford, 110

Disbrowe, Samuel, 23
Dover, treaty of, 105
Downing, Sir George, 23, 25, 103
Dryden, John, 102, 109, 110
Duke of Guise, The, play, 109
Dunbar, battle of, 12
Dundee, earl of, 76
Dunfermline, abbey of, 86
Dunfermline, dowager countess
    of, 58
Dunfermline, earl of, *see* Seton,
    Alexander
Dunfermline, lordship and
    regality of, 95
Dutch war, 101, 112

Edinburgh, bishop of, 92
Edinburgh Castle, 55, 63
Edinburgh, College of, 20
Elcho, David, Lord, 77, 98
Elizabeth I, 5
Elliott, Gilbert of Stobs, 28, 30,
    32–3, 34, 38, 50, 52
Engagement, the, 12, 15, 16, 21, 80
Engager army, 80
English government, 16–17
entail, earl of Leven's, 76
entail, Earl Francis', 58, 64, 68–72, 76,
    79, 82–84, 87, 89, 90, 95, 121
Erroll, earl of, 34, 38
Erroll, house of, 19
Evelyn, John, 62, 96, 98, 99, 108,
    109, 117

Fawkes, Guy, 107
Fife, synod of, 38–9
Fox, Sir Stephen, 97, 100, 114,
    117, 119–121
France, 105, 114
Freuchie, laird of, 76

Gazette, the, 116
Gibbons, Grinling, 122

Gilmour, Sir John, 23, 29, 34, 49, 53, 64–68, 71, 83, 85–88, 90
Glencairn, Lord Chancellor, 71, 85–88, 90
Great Russell Street, 96, 115
'Greysteel', *see* Montgomery, Alexander
Guthrie, James, 63, 93
Gwyn, Nell, 98, 103, 114, 123

Haddington, earl of, 123
Halifax, earl of, 116
Hamilton, Anne, duchess of, 76, 122
Hamilton, duke of, 61, 80, 122
Harden, *see* Scott, Sir William of Harden
Hawick, barony of, 119
Hay, John, Lord Yester, earl of Tweeddale, 10, 11, 17–20, 22–26, 28–31, 34–40, 42, 44, 48, 49, 51, 53–59, 63–66, 70–73, 76, 79, 81, 82, 86, 91–95, 98, 99, 114, 122, *see also* debt, Tweeddale
Hay, Margaret, 20
Haychesters, Lord, *see* Scott, Gideon
Hays of Yester, 19
Hedge Lane, 72, 99, 100, 104, 117
Henrietta Maria, 65, 73, 104, 105
Holland, 119
Horace, play, 109
horseracing, 101n., 106, 108n., 110
hunting, 88, 107
Huntly, marquis of, 17
Hyde, Anne, duchess of York, 108
Hyde, Henry, earl of Clarendon, 1, 2, 60, 70

Indian Emperor, play, 109

James, earl of Dalkeith, 3
James IV, King, 73

James V, King, 66
James VI and I, King, 5, 62, 73, 80, 106–7
James VII and II, King, 1, 2, 3, 95, 117, 119, memoirs of, 99
Johnston, Archibald of Wariston, 41

Kéroualle, Louise de, 107
King Arthur, 110
'king's evil', the, 114
kingship, 62, 63
Kirkcaldy, presbytery of, 33–4
Kirke, Moll, 110, 112
Kneller, Sir Godfrey, 110
Konigsmark, Count, 74

Lambert, General John, 30, 45, 49
Lamont, John, diarist, 14, 50, 76
Langholm, barony of, 8
Lauderdale, countess of, 94
Lauderdale, earl of, *see* Maitland, John
Lauderdale estates, 94
Lawrence, Henry, president of the Protector's council, 24–5
Lely, Peter, 104, 110
Leopold, Emperor, 117
Leslie, Alexander, Lord Balgonie, 9
Leslie, Alexander, earl of Leven, 9, 76
Leslie, General Alexander, 76
Leslie, John, 7th earl of Rothes, 11, 12, 22, 26, 30, 32, 36, 39, 42–51, 54, 56–65, 67–69, 73, 76–78, 81–88, 90, 91, 98, 122
Leslie, Margaret, m.1 Francis Scott, m.2 earl of Wemyss, 9, 11–13, 15, 16, 25–37, 39, 42, 43, 45, 47–54, 56, 58–60, 63, 65–73, 76–79, 81–84, 87, 88, 91, 99, 102, 110

Leslie, Margaret, countess of Leven, 76, 77
Leven, David, earl of, 78
Liddesdale, lordship of, 8
Lincoln's Inn Fields, 104
Lindsay, John, earl of Lindsay and Crawford, 45
Lockhart, George of Carnwath, Lord Advocate, 39
London, 65, 67, 80, 86, 92, 100, 105, 107, 123
lords of the articles, 52
Louis XIV, 112

Maastricht, siege of, 101
Mackenzie, George, 60
maids of honour, 108, 109
Maitland, John, 2nd earl of Lauderdale, 16, 22, 45, 47, 49, 54, 56, 57, 60, 61, 62–67, 71–73, 77, 79–94, 113
Maitland, John, of Thirlestane, 80
Mar, dowager countess of, 35
Mar, earl of, 34
Margaret Tudor, 73
marriage, 25, 30, 31, 46, 48, 59, 69, 73, 74, 76–78
marriage, Anna's, 57, 60, 63, 68, 69, 72, 73, 82, 84, 86, 97
marriage, Mary's, 35, 37, 38, 39, 47, 51, 52, 56, 64, 76, 87
marriage contract, Anna's, 70, 79, 81, 83, 85, 86, 88, 89, 91–93, 95, 114
marriage contract, Mary's, 32–34, 48, 52, 55, 58, 59, 64, 65
Mary II, 73
Mary, countess of Buccleuch, *see* Scott, Mary
Mary of Modena, Queen, 73, 108, 111, 117, 121
Mary, Queen of Scots, 15, 62, 73, 102

master of the horse, 100, 114
Melrose, lordship of, 123
Melville, Lord, 32, 73, 77, 104, 114, 115, 120, 122
Middleton, earl of, 52, 81–83, 85, 86
Modena, Mary of, Queen, 73, 108, 111, 117, 121
Monck, General, 12, 14, 17, 28, 34–37, 39, 42, 44–48, 58, 60, 84, 111, 112
Monmouth, duke of, *see* Scott, James, duke of Monmouth
Monmouth, earl of, 119, *see also* Carey, Robert
Monmouth title, 119
Montagu, Lady Jemima, 75
Montgomery, Alexander, earl of Eglinton, 7, 9, 12, 30, 34, 50, 56
Montgomery, Lady Mary, 50
Montgomery, Lord, Eglinton's son, 78
Montgomery, Margaret, 122
Montrose, marquis of, 13, 21
Moor Park, 3, 100, 113, 114, 116
Moray, earl of, 66, 76, 119
Moray, Sir Robert, 82–85, 87–91, 93
Mordaunt, Lord, 119
Morpeth, Viscount, 45, 47
Morton, earl of, 8
Mulgrave, earl of, 111, 113
Murray, Sir Gideon, of Elibank, 6
Murray, Sir James, 18
Musselburgh, lordship of, 85, 86

Needham, Eleanor, 96, 106, 115
Neidpath Castle, 21
Newburgh, earl of, 74
Newmarket, 106, 110
Nisbet, Sir John, of Dirleton, 37, 39–41, 53, 58, 67, 86
Northesk, earl of, 78

Oates, Titus, 107
Orléans, duc d', 104
Overbury, Sir Thomas, 107
Oxford, 88–91, 100

Parbroath, Lord, 56
Paris, 94
Parliament, Cavalier, 113
Parliament, English, 62, 63, 84, 92
Parliament, Protectorate, 28
Parliament, Richard Cromwell's,
    32
Parliament, Rump, 40, 41
Parliament, Scottish, 52, 79, 82–
    85, 87, 90–92, 94
Pennycuik, Alexander,
    'chirrurgian', 51
Pepys, Samuel, 65, 66, 72, 75, 96,
    99, 104, 105, 109–111
Percy, Elizabeth, 74
Philiphaugh, battle of, 21
plague, 100
Popish Plot, 97, 113
Portsmouth, 85
Pregnani, Abbé, 106
presbyterianism, 80
Preston, battle of, 211
Primrose, Sir Archibald, 18
'Prince Perkin', 98, 114, 117, 123,
    see also Scott, James, duke of
    Monmouth
Prior, Matthew, 96
privy council, 63, 82
privy council, English, 111, 113
privy council, Scottish, 111, 116,
    119
Protestantism, 112, 117n.
Purcell, William, 110

Queensberry, duke of, 95

Ranelagh, Lord, 103
rebellion in Scotland, 101, 113

rebels, 80
Reid, Alexander, 93
Restoration, the, 14
revolution of 1688, 119
Rochester, John Wilmot, earl of,
    102, 108
Roos divorce case, 75, 112
Roos, Lord and Lady, 75
Ross, Sir Thomas, 90, 99
Roxburgh, earl of, 34
royalists, 80
Royston, 107
Rye House Plot, 55, 115, 120

St. Andrews, archbishop of, 81
St. James's, 117
St. Martin's in the Fields, 96
St. Nicholas' Church, Dalkeith,
    123
Sandwich, earl of, 75
Savile, Henry, 103
Savoy, duke of, 99
Scone Palace, 45
Scotstarvit, *see* Scott, Sir John
Scott, Anna, duchess of
    Buccleuch, 1, 2, 10, 12, 15, 23,
    26, 27, 30, 33, 34, 36–38, 40–
    43, 49, 51–53, 55–59, 63, 65–
    69, 71–73, 76, 79, 85, 87, 89,
    90, 93–101, 104–121, 123
Scott, David, brother of Earl
    Francis, 6, 10, 25, 41
Scott, Francis, 2nd earl of
    Buccleuch, 6–18, 22, 23, 25, 44,
    46, 58, 71
Scott, Gideon, of Haychesters, 13,
    23–30, 32–41, 44, 47–54, 57–60,
    64, 67, 70, 92, 93
Scott, James, duke of Monmouth
    and Buccleuch, 1–3, 54, 55, 59,
    65–74, 79, 81–87, 89–91, 93, 94,
    97, 98, 100–106, 109–115, 117–
    120

Scott, Jean, Lady Tweeddale, sister of Earl Francis, 20, 31–33, 36, 58, 63, 70, 72, 73, 81, 92–95, 106

Scott, John of Gorrenberry, 28, 30, 32, 34, 38, 52, 56

Scott, John of Newburgh, 50

Scott, Sir John of Scotstarvit, 6, 11, 17, 22, 24, 28–30, 32, 34–36, 38–39, 47, 49, 50, 52, 53, 56

Scott, Lawrence of Bavielaw, 28, 32, 34, 52, 58, 68, 71

Scott, Margaret, Lady Ross, 7, 9, 12, 14

Scott, Mary, duchess of Buccleuch, daughter of Francis Scott, 13, 23, 26–30, 32–36, 38–43, 46, 49, 50, 53, 56, 57, 60, 72, 76, 78, 93

Scott, Mary, sister of Francis Scott, 10

Scott, Patrick of Langshaw, 23, 27, 28, 32, 34, 35, 48, 52, 58

Scott, Patrick of Thirlestane, 17, 24, 30, 32, 34, 38, 52, 56

Scott, Richard, 4

Scott, Sir Walter, 4, 96

Scott, Walter, Lord Scott of Buccleuch, 4, 5, 123

Scott, Walter, later earl of Tarras, 33, 35, 42, 48–50, 52–55, 57, 59, 64, 65, 69–71, 76, 94, 115

Scott, Walter of Satchells, poet, 8, 13, 91, 122

Scott, Walter, son of Lord Scott of Buccleuch, 6

Scott, William of Clerkington, 23, 27, 28, 29, 43

Scott, Sir William of Harden, 6, 11, 13, 17, 24, 27–30, 32, 34, 38, 50, 51, 53

Scotts of Buccleuch, 4

Sedgemoor, battle of, 117

Seton, Alexander, earl of Dunfermline, 20, 22, 80

Seton, Charles, 2nd earl of Dunfermline, 20, 22, 41, 80, 95

Seton House, 20

Seton, Jean, 20

Shadwell, Thomas, 110

Shaftesbury, earl of, 49, 63, 97, 113, 115

Sharp, William, 81

Sherard, Alice, 74

Sheriffhall, 14, 32

Sidney, Henry, 97, 98

Signet office, 47

Smith, James, architect, 122

Solemn League and Covenant, 7, 13

Somerset, duke of, 74, 75, 104

Southwold Bay, naval battle, 101

Stewart, Anne, Princess, 109, 117

Stewart, James, duke of York, 101, 110–113, 116, *see also* James II

Stewart, Mary, Princess, 106, 108, 109

Stewart dynasty, 101

Stirling, earl of, 8

Stuart, Lady Frances, 84, 103, 108

Sutherland, earl of, 77

Sweden, 111

taking the waters, 85, 105

Tarras, earl of, *see* Scott, Walter

Test Act, 111

theatre, Restoration, 109

Thynne, Thomas, 74

Toddington, 115, 116

Tower Hill, 112

Tower of London, 116, 117

Tunbridge Wells, 85

tutors to Anna and Mary Scott, 11, 14, 16–18, 23–29, 38, 47, 50, 52, 58–60, 64, 71, 79

tutors to Francis Scott, 6, 8

Tweeddale, Lady, *see* Scott, Jean

Tweeddale, Lord, *see* Hay, John

Union of Parliaments, 1707, 123
United Provinces, the, 115, 117

Verney, Sir Edmund, 75
Vernon, James, 110

Wallace, Sir Thomas, 66, 67, 69
Waller, Elizabeth, 106
Walter, Lucy, 99, 112
Wandesford, Alice, 75
wardship, 8, 46–48, 56, 57, 67, 68
Wellwood, James, 61
Wemyss, 77, 78
Wemyss Castle, 14, 32, 34, 42, 50,
    65, 79
Wemyss, David, earl of, 14–16,
    18, 24, 25, 30, 32–34, 37–39, 41,
    42, 48, 50, 51, 53, 56–59, 72,
    77–79, 82, 84, 90, 120
Wemyss, James, 78
Wemyss, Lady, *see* Leslie,
    Margaret
Wentworth, Lady Henrietta, 1,
    96, 97, 114–116, 118

Whetstone Park, 104
Whitehall, Palace of, 72, 81, 100,
    103, 105–107, 110, 114, 115,
    117, 119
wildfowling, 105
Wilkie, Henry, 34
will of Countess Mary, 42, 50, 51,
    56
will of Earl Francis, 10, 11, 13, 28,
    52, 58, 71
William II of Orange, 73, 112,
    113, 117
William III, 61, 95, 108, 119, 121
Wilmot, John, earl of Rochester,
    see Rochester
Winton, earl of, 73
women, place of at court, 106–7
Worcester, battle of, 12, 16, 45,
    61, 80, 82, 102
Wycherley, William, 108

Yester House, 19, 49, 63, 122
Yester, Lady, 94
Yester, Lord, 211, 30, 93
York, duke of, 66, 97, 99,
    105